THE

BOOK OF PLEASURES:

CONTAINING

THE PLEASURES OF HOPE,

BY THOMAS CAMPBELL;

THE PLEASURES OF MEMORY,

BY SAMUEL ROGERS;

AND THE

PLEASURES OF IMAGINATION,

BY MARK AKENSIDE.

NEW YORK:
PUBLISHED BY CLARK & AUSTIN,
NO. 205 BROADWAY.
1851.

PREFACE.

SEPARATE editions of the three poems com prising this volume, in a style proportioned to the high estimation in which they are held, have long been required in this country; and their coincidence of design, in several important respects, renders the expediency of their united publication very obvious. Discrepancies are, indeed, observable in the manner in which the three bards have executed their several tasks; yet the delineation of Humanity has been their common aim; and the combined results of their labours afford us a rich and beautiful portraiture of her distinguishing attributes—Hope, Imagination, and Memory. The pictures are not, indeed, complete or perfect. Akenside has been justly censured for not more distinctly alluding to one of the sublimest themes towards which ideality tends—the immortality of the soul; and no reader of just taste can fail to lament his untimely death, whereby his greatest production was bereft of the finishing touches he designed to bestow upon it. Campbell's extreme devotion to mere diction, and the absence of true originality in the poetry of Rogers, have very properly furnished occasions for critical objection. Yet so interesting and delightful are the prominent features of these poems, that we wonder not that they are enshrined amid the household lore of English literature. Genuine poetical talent characterizes them, if not equally, yet in no ordinary degree. The Book of Pleasures, therefore, is eminently calculated to subserve the great end of Poetry. A spirit of humanity, a grateful recognition of religious truth, and a holy love of nature, pervade its pages. The images it presents are fitted to refine as well as delight; the ideas it affords are suggestive as well as pleasing; for the subjects to which it is devoted, and the gratifications to which it ministers, are not extrinsic but spiritual—pertaining to, and addressing those inward and quenchless fountains of pleasure—Hope, Imagination, and Memory.

PHILADELPHIA, *September*, 1835.

CONTENTS.

CAMPBELL'S

PLEASURES OF HOPE.

PART I.

ANALYSIS OF PART I.

The poem opens with a comparison between the beauty of remote objects in a landscape, and those ideal scenes of felicity which the imagination delights to contemplate—the influence of anticipation upon the other passions is next delineated—an allusion is made to the well-known fiction in pagan tradition that, when all the guardian deities of mankind abandoned the world, Hope alone was left behind—the consolations of this passion in situations of danger and distress—the seaman on his midnight watch—the soldier marching into battle—allusion to the interesting adventures of Byron.

The inspiration of Hope, as it actuates the efforts of genius, whether in the department of science or of taste—domestic felicity, how intimately connected with views of future happiness—picture of a mother watching her infant when asleep—pictures of the prisoner, the maniac, and the wanderer.

From the consolations of individual misery, a transition is made to prospects of political improvement in the future state of society—the wide field that is yet open for the progress of humanizing arts among uncivilized nations—from these views of amelioration of society, and the extension of liberty and truth over despotic and barbarous countries, by melancholy contrast of ideas we are led to reflect upon the hard fate of a brave people, recently conspicuous in their struggles for independence—description of the capture of Warsaw, of the last contest of the oppressors and the oppressed, and the massacre of the Polish patriots at the bridge of Prague—apostrophe to the self-interested enemies of human improvement—the wrongs of Africa—the barbarous policy of Europeans in India—prophecy in the Hindoo mythology of the expected descent of the Deity, to redress the miseries of their race, and to take vengeance on the violators of justice and mercy.

THE

PLEASURES OF HOPE.

PART I.

AT summer eve, when Heaven's aerial bow
Spans with bright arch the glittering hills below,
Why to yon mountain turns the musing eye,
Whose sun-bright summit mingles with the sky?
Why do those cliffs of shadowy tint appear
More sweet than all the landscape smiling near?—
'T is distance lends enchantment to the view,
And robes the mountain in its azure hue.

Thus, with delight, we linger to survey
The promised joys of life's unmeasured way;
Thus, from afar, each dim-discover'd scene
More pleasing seems than all the past hath been;
And every form, that fancy can repair
From dark oblivion, glows divinely there.

What potent spirit guides the raptured eye
To pierce the shades of dim futurity?
Can Wisdom lend, with all her heavenly power,
The pledge of Joy's anticipated hour?

Ah, no! she darkly sees the fate of man—
Her dim horizon bounded to a span;
Or, if she hold an image to the view,
'T is Nature pictured too severely true.

With thee, sweet Hope! resides the heavenly light
That pours remotest rapture on the sight:
Thine is the charm of life's bewilder'd way,
That calls each slumbering passion into play:
Waked by thy touch, I see the sister band,
On tiptoe watching, start at thy command,
And fly where'er thy mandate bids them steer,
To Pleasure's path, or Glory's bright career.

Primeval Hope, the Aonian Muses say,
When Man and Nature mourn'd their first decay;
When every form of death, and every woe,
Shot from malignant stars to earth below;
When Murder bared his arm, and rampant War
Yoked the red dragons of her iron car;
When Peace and Mercy, banish'd from the plain,
Sprung on the viewless winds to Heaven again;
All, all forsook the friendless guilty mind,
But Hope, the charmer, linger'd still behind.

Thus, while Elijah's burning wheels prepare
From Carmel's height to sweep the fields of air,
The Prophet's mantle, ere his flight began,
Dropp'd on the world—a sacred gift to man.

Auspicious Hope! in thy sweet garden grow
Wreaths for each toil, a charm for every woe:
Won by their sweets, in Nature's languid hour
The way-worn pilgrim seeks thy summer bower;
There, as the wild-bee murmurs on the wing,
What peaceful dreams thy handmaid spirits bring!
What viewless forms th' Æolian organ play,
And sweep the furrow'd lines of anxious thought away.

Angel of life! thy glittering wings explore
Earth's loneliest bounds, and ocean's wildest shore.
Lo! to the wint'ry wind the pilot yields
His bark careering o'er unfathom'd fields;
Now on Atlantic waves he rides afar,
Where Andes, giant of the western star,
With meteor standard to the winds unfurl'd,
Looks from his throne of clouds o'er half the world.

Now far he sweeps, where scarce a summer smiles,
On Behring's rocks, or Greenland's naked isles:
Cold on his midnight watch the breezes blow,
From wastes that slumber in eternal snow;
And waft, across the waves' tumultuous roar,
The wolf's long howl from Oonalaska's shore.

Poor child of danger, nursling of the storm,
Sad are the woes that wreck thy manly form!
Rocks, waves, and winds, the shatter'd bark delay;
Thy heart is sad, thy home is far away.

But Hope can here her moonlight vigils keep,
And sing to charm the spirit of the deep.
Swift as yon streamer lights the starry pole,
Her visions warm the watchman's pensive soul:
His native hills that rise in happier climes,
The grot that heard his song of other times,
His cottage-home, his bark of slender sail,
His glassy lake, and broomwood-blossom'd vale,
Rush on his thought; he sweeps before the wind,
Treads the loved shore he sigh'd to leave behind;
Meets at each step a friend's familiar face,
And flies at last to Helen's long embrace;
Wipes from her cheek the rapture-speaking tear,
And clasps, with many a sigh, his children dear!
While, long neglected, but at length caress'd,
His faithful dog salutes the smiling guest,
Points to his master's eyes (where'er they roam)
His wistful face, and whines a welcome home.

Friend of the brave! in peril's darkest hour,
Intrepid Virtue looks to thee for power;
To thee the heart its trembling homage yields,
On stormy floods, and carnage-cover'd fields,
When front to front the banner'd hosts combine,
Halt ere they close, and form the dreadful line;
When all is still on Death's devoted soil,
The march-worn soldier mingles for the toil;
As rings his glittering tube, he lifts on high
The dauntless brow, and spirit-speaking eye,

Hails in his heart the triumph yet to come,
And hears thy stormy music in the drum.

And such thy strength-inspiring aid that bore
The hardy Byron to his native shore.—*(a)*
In horrid climes, where Chiloe's tempests sweep
Tumultuous murmurs o'er the troubled deep,
'T was his to mourn misfortune's rudest shock,
Scourged by the wind, and cradled on the rock,
To wake each joyless morn, and search again
The famish'd haunts of solitary men,
Whose race, unyielding as their native storm,
Knows not a trace of Nature but the form;
Yet, at thy call, the hardy tar pursued,
Pale but intrepid, sad but unsubdued,
Pierced the deep woods, and, hailing from afar
The moon's pale planet and the northern star;
Paused at each dreary cry, unheard before,
Hyenas in the wild, and mermaids on the shore;
Till, led by thee o'er many a cliff sublime,
He found a warmer world, a milder clime,
A home to rest, a shelter to defend,
Peace and repose, a Briton and a friend! *(b)*

Congenial Hope! thy passion-kindling power,
How bright, how strong, in youth's untroubled hour
On yon proud height, with Genius hand in hand,
I see thee light, and wave thy golden wand.

"Go, Child of heaven, (thy winged words proclaim)
'T is thine to search the boundless fields of fame!
Lo! Newton, priest of Nature, shines afar,
Scans the wide world, and numbers every star!
Wilt thou, with him, mysterious rites apply,
And watch the shrine with wonder-beaming eye?
Yes, thou shalt mark, with magic art profound,
The speed of light, the circling march of sound;
With Franklin, grasp the lightning's fiery wing,
Or yield the lyre of Heaven another string. (*c*)

"The Swedish sage admires, in yonder bowers, (*d*)
His winged insects, and his rosy flowers;
Calls from their woodland haunts the savage train
With sounding horn, and counts them on the plain—
So once, at Heaven's command, the wanderers came
To Eden's shade, and heard their various name.

"Far from the world, in yon sequester'd clime,
Slow pass the sons of Wisdom, more sublime;
Calm as the fields of Heaven his sapient eye
The loved Athenian lifts to realms on high;
Admiring Plato, on his spotless page,
Stamps the bright dictates of the father sage;
'Shall Nature bound to earth's diurnal span
The fire of God, th' immortal soul of man?'

"Turn, Child of Heaven, thy rapture-lighten'd eye
To Wisdom's walk,—the sacred Nine are nigh:

Hark! from bright spires that gild the Delphian height,
From streams that wander in eternal light,
Ranged on their hill, Harmonia's daughters swell
The mingling tones of horn, and harp, and shell;
Deep from his vaults the Loxian murmurs flow, (*e*)
And Pythia's awful organ peals below.

"Beloved of Heaven! the smiling Muse shall shed
Her moonlight halo on thy beauteous head;
Shall swell thy heart to rapture unconfined,
And breathe a holy madness o'er thy mind.
I see thee roam her guardian power beneath,
And talk with spirits on the midnight heath;
Inquire of guilty wanderers whence they came,
And ask each blood-stain'd form his earthly name
Then weave in rapid verse the deeds they tell,
And read the trembling world the tales of hell.

"When Venus, throned in clouds of rosy hue,
Flings from her golden urn the vesper dew,
And bids fond man her glimmering noon employ,
Sacred to love and walks of tender joy;
A milder mood the goddess shall recall,
And soft as dew thy tones of music fall;
While Beauty's deeply-pictured smiles impart
A pang more dear than pleasure to the heart—
Warm as thy sighs shall flow the Lesbian strain,
And plead in Beauty's ear, nor plead in vain.

"Or wilt thou Orphean hymns more sacred deem
And steep thy song in Mercy's mellow stream·
To pensive drops the radiant eye beguile—
For Beauty's tears are lovelier than her smile;
On Nature's throbbing anguish pour relief,
And teach impassion'd souls the joy of grief?

"Yes; to thy tongue shall seraph words be given,
And power on earth to plead the cause of heaven:
The proud, the cold untroubled heart of stone,
That never mused on sorrow but its own,
Unlocks a generous store at thy command,
Like Horeb's rocks beneath the prophet's hand. (*f*)
The living lumber of his kindred earth,
Charm'd into soul, receives a second birth;
Feels thy dread power another heart afford,
Whose passion-touch'd harmonious strings accord
True as the circling spheres to Nature's plan;
And man, the brother, lives the friend of man!

"Bright as the pillar rose at Heaven's command,
When Israel march'd along the desert lana,
Blazed through the night on lonely wilds afar,
And told the path—a never-setting star:
So, heavenly Genius, in thy course divine,
Hope is thy star, her light is ever thine."

Propitious Power! when rankling cares annoy
The sacred home of Hymenean joy;

When doom'd to Poverty's sequester'd del ,
The wedded pair of love and virtue dwell,
Unpitied by the world, unknown to fame,
Their woes, their wishes, and their hearts the same—
Oh there, prophetic hope! thy smile bestow,
And chase the pangs that worth should never know—
There, as the parent deals his scanty store
To friendless babes, and weeps to give no more,
Tell, that his manly race shall yet assuage
Their father's wrongs, and shield his later age.
What though for him no Hybla's sweets distil,
Nor bloomy vines wave purple on the hill;
Tell, that when silent years have pass'd away,
That when his eyes grow dim, his tresses gray,
These busy hands a lovelier cot shall build,
And deck with fairer flowers his little field,
And call from Heaven propitious dews to breathe
Arcadian beauty on the barren heath;
Tell, that while Love's spontaneous smile endears
The days of peace, the sabbath of his years,
Health shall prolong to many a festive hour
The social pleasures of his humble bower

Lo! at the couch where infant beauty sleeps,
Her silent watch the mournful mother keeps;
She, while the lovely babe unconscious lies,
Smiles on her slumb'ring child with pensive eyes,
And weaves a song of melancholy joy—
"Sleep, image of thy father, sleep, my boy:

No lingering hour of sorrow shall be thine;
No sight that rends thy father's heart and mine;
Bright as his manly sire, the son shall be
In form and soul; but, ah! more blest than he!
Thy fame, thy worth, thy filial love, at last,
Shall soothe this aching heart for all the past—
With many a smile my solitude repay,
And chase the world's ungenerous scorn away.

"And say, when summon'd from the world and thee,
I lay my head beneath the willow tree,
Wilt *thou*, sweet mourner! at my stone appear,
And soothe my parted spirit lingering near?
Oh, wilt thou come, at evening hour, to shed
The tears of Memory o'er my narrow bed;
With aching temples on thy hand reclined,
Muse on the last farewell I leave behind,
Breathe a deep sigh to winds that murmur low,
And think on all my love, and all my woe?"

So speaks affection, ere the infant eye
Can look regard, or brighten in reply;
But when the cherub lip hath learnt to claim
A mother's ear by that endearing name;
Soon as the playful innocent can prove
A tear of pity, or a smile of love,
Or cons his murmuring task beneath her care,
Or lisps with holy look his evening prayer,

Or gazing, mutely pensive, sits to hear
The mournful ballad warbled in his ear;
How fondly looks admiring Hope the while,
At every artless tear, and every smile!
How glows the joyous parent to descry
A guileless bosom, true to sympathy!

Where is the troubled heart, consign'd to share
Tumultuous toils, or solitary care,
Unblest by visionary thoughts that stray
To count the joys of Fortune's better day!
Lo, nature, life, and liberty relume
The dim-eyed tenant of the dungeon gloom,
A long-lost friend, or hapless child restored,
Smiles at his blazing hearth and social board;
Warm from his heart the tears of rapture flow,
And virtue triumphs o'er remember'd woe.

Chide not his peace, proud Reason! nor destroy
The shadowy forms of uncreated joy,
That urge the lingering tide of life, and pour
Spontaneous slumber on his midnight hour.

Hark! the wild maniac sings, to chide the gale
That wafts so slow her lover's distant sail;
She, sad spectatress, on the wintry shore
Watch'd the rude surge his shroudless corse that bore,
Knew the pale form, and, shrieking in amaze,
Clasp'd her cold hands, and fix'd her maddening gaze:

Poor widow'd wretch! 't was there she wept in vain
Till memory fled her agonizing brain:—
But Mercy gave, to charm the sense of woe,
Ideal peace, that truth could ne'er bestow;
Warm on her heart the joys of Fancy beam,
And aimless Hope delights her darkest dream.

Oft when yon moon hath climb'd the midnight sky,
And the lone sea-bird wakes its wildest cry,
Piled on the steep, her blazing fagots burn
To hail the bark that never can return;
And still she waits, but scarce forbears to weep,
That constant love can linger on the deep.

And, mark the wretch, whose wanderings never knew
The world's regard, that soothes, though half untrue,
Whose erring heart the lash of sorrow bore,
But found not pity when it err'd no more.
Yon friendless man, at whose dejected eye
Th' unfeeling proud one looks—and passes by;
Condemn'd on Penury's barren path to roam,
Scorn'd by the world, and left without a home—
E'en he, at evening, should he chance to stray
Down by the hamlet's hawthorn-scented way,
Where, round the cot's romantic glade, are seen
The blossom'd bean-field, and the sloping green,
Leans o'er its humble gate, and thinks the while—
Oh! that for me some home like this would smile,

Some hamlet shade, to shield my sickly form,
Health in the breeze, and shelter in the storm!
There should my hand no stinted boon assign
To wretched hearts with sorrow such as mine!
That generous wish can soothe unpitied care,
And Hope half mingles with the poor man's prayer

Hope! when I mourn, with sympathizing mind,
The wrongs of fate, the woes of human kind,
Thy blissful omens bid my spirit see
The boundless fields of rapture yet to be,
I watch the wheels of Nature's mazy plan,
And learn the future by the past of man.

Come, bright Improvement! on the car of Time,
And rule the spacious world from clime to clime;
Thy handmaid arts shall every wild explore,
Trace every wave, and culture every shore.
On Erie's banks, where tigers steal along,
And the dread Indian chants a dismal song,
Where human fiends on midnight errands walk,
And bathe in brains the murderous tomahawk;
There shall the flocks on thymy pasture stray,
And shepherds dance at Summer's opening day;
Each wandering genius of the lonely glen
Shall start to view the glittering haunts of men;
And silent watch, on woodland heights around,
The village curfew, as it tolls profound.

In Libyan groves, where damned rites are done,
That bathe the rocks in blood, and veil the sun,

Truth shall arrest the murderous arm profane,
Wild Obi flies (*i*)—the veil is rent in twain.

Where barb'rous hordes on Scythian mountains roam,
Truth, Mercy, Freedom, yet shall find a home;
Where'er degraded Nature bleeds and pines,
From Guinea's coast to Sibir's dreary mines, (*g*)
Truth shall pervade th' unfathom'd darkness there,
And light the dreadful features of despair.—
Hark! the stern captive spurns his heavy load,
And asks the image back that Heaven bestow'd:
Fierce in his eyes the fire of valour burns,
And, as the slave departs, the man returns.

Oh! sacred Truth! thy triumph ceased awhile,
And Hope, thy sister, ceased with thee to smile,
When leagued Oppression pour'd to northern wars
Her whisker'd pandours and her fierce hussars,
Waved her dread standard to the breeze of morn,
Peal'd her loud drum, and twang'd her trumpet horn;
Tumultuous horror brooded o'er her van,
Presaging wrath to Poland—and to man! (*h*)

Warsaw's last champion from her height survey'd,
Wide o'er the fields, a waste of ruin laid,—
Oh! Heaven! he cried, my bleeding country save;
Is there no hand on high to shield the brave?
Yet, though destruction sweep these lovely plains,
Rise, fellow-men! our country yet remains!

By that dread name, we wave the sword on high,
And swear for her to live!—with her to die!

He said, and on the rampart-heights array'd
His trusty warriors, few, but undismay'd!
Firm-paced and slow, a horrid front they form,
Still as the breeze, but dreadful as the storm;
Low, murmuring sounds along their banners fly,
Revenge, or death,—the watchword and reply;
Then peal'd the notes omnipotent to charm,
And the loud tocsin toll'd their last alarm!—

In vain, alas! in vain, ye gallant few!
From rank to rank your volley'd thunder flew:—
Oh! bloodiest picture in the book of Time,
Sarmatia fell, unwept, without a crime;
Found not a generous friend, a pitying foe,
Strength in her arms, nor mercy in her woe!
Dropt from her nerveless grasp the shatter'd spear,
Closed her bright eye, and curb'd her high career!—
Hope, for a season, bade the world farewell,
And Freedom shriek'd—as Kosciusko fell.

The sun went down, nor ceased the carnage there,
Tumultuous murder shook the midnight air—
On Prague's proud arch the fires of ruin glow,
His blood-dyed waters murmuring far below;
The storm prevails, the ramparts yield a way,
Bursts the wild cry of horror and dismay;

Hark! as the smouldering piles with thunder fall,
A thousand shrieks for hopeless mercy call!
Earth shook—red meteors flash'd along the sky,
And conscious Nature shudder'd at the cry!

Oh! Righteous Heaven! ere Freedom found a grave,
Why slept thy sword, omnipotent to save?
Where was thine arm, O Vengeance! where thy rod,
That smote the foes of Zion and of God,
That crush'd proud Ammon, when his iron car
Was yoked in wrath, and thunder'd from afar?
Where was the storm that slumber'd till the host
Of blood-stain'd Pharaoh left their trembling coast?
Then bade the deep in wild commotion flow,
And heaved an ocean on their march below?

Departed spirits of the mighty dead!
Ye that at Marathon and Leuctra bled!
Friends of the world! restore your swords to man,
Fight in his sacred cause, and lead the van
Yet for Sarmatia's tears of blood atone,
And make her arm puissant as your own!
Oh! once again to Freedom's cause return
The patriot TELL—the BRUCE of *Bannockburn!*

Yes! thy proud lords, unpitying band! shall see
That man hath yet a soul—and dare be free;

A little while, along thy saddening plains,
The starless night of desolation reigns;
Truth shall restore the light by Nature given,
And, like Prometheus, bring the fire of Heaven!
Prone to the dust Oppression shall be hurl'd,—
Her name, her nature, wither'd from the world!

Ye that the rising moon invidious mark,
And hate the light—because your deeds are dark;
Ye that expanding truth invidious view,
And think, or wish the song of Hope untrue!
Perhaps your little hands presume to span
The march of Genius, and the powers of Man;
Perhaps ye watch, at Pride's unhallow'd shrine,
Her victims, newly slain, and thus divine:—
"Here shall thy triumph, Genius, cease; and here,
Truth, Science, Virtue, close your short career."

Tyrants! in vain ye trace the wizard ring;
In vain ye limit Mind's unwearied spring:
What! can ye lull the winged winds asleep,
Arrest the rolling world, or chain the deep?
No:—the wild wave contemns your sceptred hand;—
It roll'd not back when Canute gave command!

Man! can thy doom no brighter soul allow?
Still must thou live a blot on Nature's brow?
Shall War's polluted banner ne'er be furl'd?
Shall crimes and tyrants cease but with the world?

What! are thy triumphs, sacred Truth, belied?
Why then hath Plato lived—or Sidney died?

Ye fond adorers of departed fame,
Who warm at Scipio's worth, or Tully's name;
Ye that, in fancied vision, can admire
The sword of Brutus, and the Theban lyre!
Wrapt in historic ardour, who adore
Each classic haunt, and well-remember'd shore,
Where Valour tuned, amid her chosen throng,
The Thracian trumpet and the Spartan song;
Or, wandering thence, behold the later charms
Of England's glory, and Helvetia's arms!
See Roman fire in Hampden's bosom swell,
And fate and freedom in the shaft of Tell!
Say, ye fond zealots to the worth of yore,
Hath Valour left the world—to live no more?
No more shall Brutus bid a tyrant die,
And sternly smile with vengeance in his eye?
Hampden no more, when suffering Freedom calls,
Encounter fate, and triumph as he falls?
Nor Tell disclose, through peril and alarm,
The might that slumbers in a peasant's arm?

Yes! in that generous cause for ever strong,
The patriot's virtue, and the poet's song,
Still, as the tide of ages rolls away,
Shall charm the world, unconscious of decay!

Yes! there are hearts, prophetic Hope may trust,
That slumber yet in uncreated dust,

Ordain'd to fire th' adoring sons of earth
With every charm of wisdom and of worth;
Ordain'd to light, with intellectual day,
The mazy wheels of Nature as they play,
Or, warm with Fancy's energy, to glow,
And rival all but Shakspeare's name below!

And say, supernal Powers! who deeply scan
Heaven's dark decrees, unfathom'd yet by man,
When shall the world call down, to cleanse her shame,
That embryo spirit, yet without a name,—
That friend of Nature, whose avenging hands
Shall burst the Libyan's adamantine bands?
Who, sternly marking on his native soil,
The blood, the tears, the anguish, and the toil,
Shall bid each righteous heart exult, to see
Peace to the slave, and vengeance on the free!

Yet, yet, degraded men! th' expected day
That breaks your bitter cup, is far away;
Trade, wealth, and fashion, ask you still to bleed,
And holy men give scripture for the deed;
Scourged and debased, no Briton stoops to save
A wretch, a coward; yes, because a slave!

Eternal Nature! when thy giant hand
Had heaved the floods, and fix'd the trembling land,
When life sprung startling at thy plastic call,
Endless her forms, and Man the lord of all;

Say, was that lordly form inspired by thee
To wear eternal chains, and bow the knee?
Was man ordain'd the slave of man to toil,
Yoked with the brutes, and fetter'd to the soil;
Weigh'd in a tyrant's balance with his gold?
No!—Nature stamp'd us in a heavenly mould?
She bade no wretch his thankless labour urge,
Nor, trembling, take the pittance and the scourge!
No homeless Libyan, on the stormy deep,
To call upon his country's name, and weep!

Lo! once in triumph on his boundless plain,
The quiver'd chief of Congo loved to reign!
With fires proportion'd to his native sky,
Strength in his arm, and lightning in his eye!
Scour'd with wild feet his sun-illumined zone,
The spear, the lion, and the woods his own!
Or led the combat, bold without a plan,
An artless savage, but a fearless man!

The plunderer came:—alas! no glory smiles
For Congo's chief on yonder Indian isles!
For ever fallen! no son of Nature now,
With Freedom charter'd on his manly brow;
Faint, bleeding, bound, he weeps the night away,
And, when the sea-wind wafts the dewless day,
Starts, with a bursting heart, for ever more
To curse the sun that lights their guilty shore.

The shrill horn blew! (*k*) at that alarum knell
His guardian angel took a last farewell!
That funeral dirge to darkness hath resign'd
The fiery grandeur of a generous mind!—
Poor fetter'd man! I hear thee whispering low
Unhallow'd vows to Guilt, the child of Woe!
Friendless thy heart! and, canst thou harbour there
A wish but death—a passion but despair?

The widow'd Indian, when her lord expires,
Mounts the dread pile, and braves the funeral fires!
So falls the heart at Thraldom's bitter sigh!
So Virtue dies, the spouse of Liberty!

But not to Libya's barren climes alone,
To Chili, or the wild Siberian zone,
Belong the wretched heart and haggard eye,
Degraded worth, and poor misfortune's sigh!
Ye orient realms, where Ganges' waters run!
Prolific fields! dominions of the sun!
How long your tribes have trembled, and obey'd!
How long was Timour's iron sceptre sway'd! (*l*)
Whose marshall'd hosts, the lions of the plain,
From Scythia's northern mountains to the main,
Raged o'er your plunder'd shrines and altars bare,
With blazing torch and gory scimitar,—
Stunn'd with the cries of death each gentle gale,
And bathed in blood the verdure of the vale!
Yet could no pangs the immortal spirit tame,
When Brama's children perish'd for his name;

The martyr smiled beneath avenging power,
And braved the tyrant in his torturing hour!

When Europe sought your subject realms to gain,
And stretch'd her giant sceptre o'er the main,
Taught her proud barks their winding way to shape,
And braved the stormy spirit of the Cape; (*m*)
Children of Brama! then was Mercy nigh
To wash the stain of blood's eternal dye?
Did Peace descend, to triumph and to save,
When free-born Britons cross'd the Indian wave?
Ah, no!—to more than Rome's ambition true,
The Nurse of Freedom gave it not to you!
She the bold route of Europe's guilt began,
And, in the march of nations, led the van!

Rich in the gems of India's gaudy zone,
And plunder piled from kingdoms not their own,
Degenerate Trade! thy minions could despise
The heart-born anguish of a thousand cries;
Could lock, with impious hands, their teeming store,
While famish'd nations died along the shore; (*n*)
Could mock the groans of fellow-men, and bear
The curse of kingdoms peopled with despair!
Could stamp disgrace on man's polluted name,
And barter, with their gold, eternal shame!

But hark! as bow'd to earth the Bramin kneels,
From heavenly climes propitious thunder peals!

Of India's fate her guardian spirits tell,
Prophetic murmurs breathing on the shell,
And solemn sounds, that awe the listening mind,
Roll on the azure paths of every wind.

Foes of mankind! (her guardian spirits say)
Revolving ages bring the bitter day,
When Heaven's unerring arm shall fall on you,
And blood for blood these Indian plains bedew;
Nine times have Brama's wheels of lightning hurl'd
His awful presence o'er the alarmed world! (*o*)
Nine times hath Guilt, through all his giant frame,
Convulsive trembled as the Mighty came!
Nine times hath suffering Mercy spared in vain—
But Heaven shall burst her starry gates again:
He comes! dread Brama shakes the sunless sky
With murmuring wrath, and thunders from on high!
Heaven's fiery horse, beneath his warrior form,
Paws the light clouds, and gallops on the storm!
Wide waves his flickering sword, his bright arms glow
Like summer suns, and light the world below!
Earth, and her trembling isles in Ocean's bed,
Are shook, and Nature rocks beneath his tread.

"To pour redress on India's injured realm,
The oppressor to dethrone, the proud to whelm;
To chase destruction from her plunder'd shore,
With arts and arms that triumph'd once before,

The tenth Avater comes! at Heaven's command
Shall Seriswattee (*p*) wave her hallow'd wand!
And Camdeo bright! and Genesa sublime,
Shall bless with joy their own propitious clime!—
Come, Heavenly Powers! primeval peace restore!
Love!—Mercy!—Wisdom! rule for ever more!"

NOTES

TO

PLEASURES OF HOPE.

PART I.

Note (*a*) And such thy strength-inspiring aid that bore
The hardy Byron to his native shore.

THE following picture of his own distress, given by Byron in his simple and interesting narrative, justifies the description in page 13.

After relating the barbarity of the Indian cacique to his child, he proceeds thus:—"A day or two after, we put to sea again, and crossed the great bay I mentioned we had been at the bottom of when we first hauled away to the westward. The land here was very low and sandy, and something like the mouth of a river which discharged itself into the sea, and which had been taken no notice of by us before, as it was so shallow that the Indians were obliged to take every thing out of their canoes, and carry it over land. We row'd up the river four or five leagues, and then took into a branch of it that ran first to the eastward, and then to the northward; here it became much narrower, and the stream excessively rapid, so that we gained but little way, though we wrought very hard. At night we landed upon its banks, and had a most uncomfortable lodging, it being a perfect swamp; and we had nothing to cover us, though it rained excessively The Indians were little better off than we, as there was no wood here to make their wigwams; so that all they could do was to prop up the bark which they carry in the bottom of their canoes, and shelter themselves as well as they could to the leeward of it. Knowing the difficulties they had to encounter here, they had provided themselves with some seal, but we had not a morsel to eat, after the heavy fatigues of the day, excepting a sort of root we saw the Indians make use of, which was very disagreeable to the taste. We laboured all next day against the stream, and fared as we had done the day before. The next day brought us to the carrying place. Here was plenty of wood, but nothing to be got for sustenance. We passed this night as we had frequently done, under a tree; but what we suffered at this time is not easy to be expressed. I had been three days at the oar, without any kind of nourishment, except the wretched root above mentioned. I had no shirt, for it had rotted off by bits. All my clothes consisted of a short grieko, (something like a bear-skin,) a piece of red cloth which had once been a waistcoat, and a ragged pair of trowsers, without shoes or stockings."

Note (*b.*) A Briton and a friend.

Don Patricio Gedd, a Scotch physician in one of the Spanish settlements, hospitably relieved Byron and his wretched associates, of which the Commodore speaks in the warmest terms of gratitude.

Note (*c.*) Or yield the lyre of heaven another string.

The seven strings of Apollo's harp were the symbolical representation of the seven planets. Herschel, by discovering an eighth, might be said to add another string to the instrument.

Note (*d.*) The Swedish sage. Linnæus.

Note (*e.*) Deep from his vaults the Loxian murmurs flow.

Loxias is a name frequently given to Apollo by Greek writers: it is met with more than once in the Chœphoræ of Æschylus.

Note (*f.*) Unlocks a generous store at thy command,
Like Horeb's rock beneath the prophet's hand.

See Exodus, chap. xvii. 3, 5, 6.

Note (*i.*) Wild Obi flies.

Among the negroes of the West Indies, Obi, or Obiah, is the name of a magical power, which is believed by them to affect the object of its malignity with dismal calamities. Such a belief must undoubtedly have been deduced from the superstitious mythology of their kinsmen on the coast of Africa. I have therefore personified Obi as the evil spirit of the African, although the history of the African tribes mentions the evil spirit of their religious creed by a different appellation.

Note (*g.*) Sibir's dreary mines.

Mr. Bell of Antermony, in his travels through Siberia, informs us that the name of the country is universally pronounced Sibir by the Russians.

Note (*h.*) Presaging wrath to Poland—and to man!

The history of the partition of Poland, of the massacre in the suburbs of Warsaw, and on the bridge of Prague, the triumphant entry of Suwarrow into the Polish capital, and the insult offered to human nature, by the blasphemous thanks offered up to Heaven, for victories obtained over men fighting in the sacred cause of liberty, by murderers and oppressors, are events generally known.

Note (*k.*) The shrill horn blew.

The negroes in the West Indies are summoned to their morning work by a shell or horn.

Note (*l.*) How long was Timour's iron sceptre sway'd?

To elucidate this passage, I shall subjoin a quotation from the Preface to letters from a Hindoo Rajah, a work of elegance and celebrity.

"The impostor of Mecca had established, as one of the principles of his doctrine, the merit of extending it, either by persuasion, or the sword, to all parts of the earth. How steadily this injunction was adhered to by his followers, and with what success it was pursued, is well known to all who are in the least conversant in history.

"The same overwhelming torrent which had inundated the greater part of Africa, burst its way into the very heart of Europe, and covered many kingdoms of Asia with unbounded desolation, directed its baleful course to the flourishing provinces of Hindostan. Here these fierce and hardy adventurers, whose only improvement had been in the science of destruction, who added the fury of fanaticism to the ravages of war, found the great end of their conquests opposed by objects which neither the ardour of their persevering zeal, nor savage barbarity could surmount. Multitudes were sacrificed by the cruel hand of religious persecution, and whole countries were deluged in blood, in the vain hope, that by the destruction of a part, the remainder might be persuaded, or terrified, into the profession of Mahomedanism; but all these sanguinary efforts were ineffectual; and at length, be ing fully convinced, that though they might extirpate, they could never hope to convert any number of the Hindoos, they relinquished the impracticable idea, with which they had entered upon their career of conquest, and contented themselves with the acquirement of the civil dominion and almost universal empire of Hindostan."——*Letters from a Hindoo Rajah, by Eliza Hamilton.*

Note (*m.*) And braved the stormy spirit of the Cape.

See the description of the Cape of Good Hope, translated from Camoens, by Mickle.

Note (*n.*) While famish'd nations died along the shore.

The following account of the British conduct, and its consequences, in Bengal, will afford a sufficient idea of the fact alluded to in this passage. After describing the monopoly of salt, betel-nut, and tobacco, the historian proceeds thus:—"Money in this current came but by drops; it could not quench the thirst of those who waited in India to receive it. An expedient, such as it was, remained to quicken its pace. The natives could live with little salt, but could not want food. Some of the agents saw themselves well situated for collecting the rice into stores: they did so. They knew the Gentoos would rather die than violate the principles of their religion by eating flesh. The alternative would therefore be between giving what they had or dying. The inhabitants sunk;—they that cultivated the land, and saw the harvest at the disposal of others, planted in doubt—scarcity ensued. Then the monopoly was easier managed—sickness ensued. In some districts the languid living left the bodies of their numerous dead unburied."——*Short History of English Transactions in the East Indies*, page 145.

Note (*o.*) Nine times hath Brama's wheels of lightning hurl'd
His awful presence o'er the prostrate world!

Among the sublime fictions of the Hindoo mythology, it is one article of belief, that the Deity Brama has descended nine times upon the world in various forms, and that he is yet to appear a tenth time, in the figure of a warrior upon a white horse, to cut off all incorrigible offenders. Avater is the word used to express his descent.

Note (*p.*) And Camdeo bright, and Genesa sublime.

Camdeo is the God of Love, in the mythology of the Hindoos. Genesa and Seriswattee correspond to the pagan deities Janus and Minerva.

4

CAMPBELL'S

PLEASURES OF HOPE.

PART II.

ANALYSIS OF PART II.

Apostrophe to the power of Love—its intimate connexion with generous and social Sensibility—allusion to that beautiful passage in the beginning of the book of Genesis, which represents the happiness of Paradise itself incomplete, till love was superadded to its other blessings—the dreams of future felicity which a lively imagination is apt to cherish, when Hope is animated by refined attachment—this disposition to combine, in one imaginary scene of residence, all that is pleasing in our estimate of happiness, compared to the skill of the great artist, who personified perfect beauty, in the picture of Venus, by an assemblage of the most beautiful features he could find—a summer and winter evening described, as they may be supposed to arise in the mind of one who wishes, with enthusiasm, for the union of friendship and retirement.

Hope and Imagination inseparable agents—even in those contemplative moments when our imagination wanders beyond the boundaries of this world, our minds are not unattended with an impression that we shall some day have a wider and distinct prospect of the universe, instead of the partial glimpse we now enjoy.

The last and most sublime influence of Hope, is the concluding topic of the Poem,—the predominance of a belief in a future state over the terrors attendant on dissolution—the baneful influence of that sceptical philosophy which bars us from such comforts—allusion to the fate of a suicide—Episode of Conrad and Ellenore—Conclusion.

THE

PLEASURES OF HOPE.

PART II.

In joyous youth, what soul hath never known
Thought, feeling, taste, harmonious to its own?
Who hath not paused while Beauty's pensive eye
Ask'd from his heart the homage of a sigh?
Who hath not own'd, with rapture-smitten frame,
The power of grace, the magic of a name?

There be, perhaps, who barren hearts avow,
Cold as the rocks on Torneo's hoary brow;
There be, whose loveless wisdom never fail'd,
In self-adoring pride securely mail'd;
But, triumph not, ye peace-enamour'd few!
Fire, Nature, Genius, never dwelt with you!
For you no fancy consecrates the scene
Where rapture utter'd vows, and wept between;
'T is yours, unmoved to sever and to meet;
No pledge is sacred, and no home is sweet!

Who that would ask a heart to dullness wed,
The waveless calm, the slumber of the dead?

No: the wild bliss of Nature needs alloy,
And care and sorrow fan the fire of joy!
And say, without our hopes, without our fears,
Without the home that plighted love endears,
Without the smiles from partial beauty won,
O! what were man?—a world without a sun!

Till Hymen brought his love-delighted hour,
There dwelt no joy in Eden's rosy bower!
In vain the viewless seraph lingering there,
At starry midnight charm'd the silent air;
In vain the wild-bird caroll'd on the steep,
To hail the sun, slow-wheeling from the deep;
In vain, to soothe the solitary shade,
Aerial notes in mingling measure play'd;
The summer wind that shook the spangled tree,
The whispering wave, the murmur of the bee;—
Still slowly pass'd the melancholy day,
And still the stranger wist not where to stray,—
The world was sad!—the garden was a wild!
And Man, the hermit, sigh'd—till Woman smiled!

True, the sad power to generous hearts may bring
Delirious anguish on his fiery wing!
Barr'd from delight by Fate's untimely hand,
By wealthless lot, or pitiless command!
Or doom'd to gaze on beauties that adorn
The smile of triumph, or the frown of scorn;
While Memory watches o'er the sad review
Of joys that faded like the morning dew!

Peace may depart—and life and nature seem
A barren path—a wildness, and a dream!

But, can the noble mind for ever brood,
The willing victim of a weary mood,
On heartless cares that squander life away,
And cloud young Genius brightening into day?
Shame to the coward thought that e'er betray'd
The noon of manhood to a myrtle shade! (*a*)
If Hope's creative spirit cannot raise
One trophy sacred to thy future days,
Scorn the dull crowd that haunt the gloomy shrine
Of hopeless love to murmur and repine!
But, should a sigh of milder mood express
Thy heart-warm wishes, true to happiness,
Should Heaven's fair harbinger delight to pour
Her blissful visions on thy pensive hour,
No tear to blot thy memory's pictured page,
No fears but such as fancy can assuage;
Though thy wild heart some hapless hour may miss,
The peaceful tenour of unvaried bliss,
(For love pursues an ever-devious race,
True to the winding lineaments of grace;)
Yet still may Hope her talisman employ
To snatch from Heaven anticipated joy,
And all her kindred energies impart
That burn the brightest in the purest heart!

When first the Rhodian's mimic art array'd
The queen of Beauty in her Cyprian shade,

The happy master mingled on his piece
Each look that charm'd him in the fair of Greece!
To faultless Nature true, he stole a grace
From every finer form and sweeter face!
And, as he sojourn'd on the Ægean isles,
Woo'd all their love, and treasured all their smiles!
Then glow'd the tints, pure, precious, and refined,
And mortal charms seem'd heavenly when combined.
Love on the picture smiled! Expression pour'd
Her mingling spirit there—and Greece adored!

So thy fair hand, enamour'd Fancy! gleans
The treasured pictures of a thousand scenes;
Thy pencil traces on the Lover's thought
Some cottage-home, from towns and toil remote,
Where Love and Lore may claim alternate hours,
With Peace embosom'd in Idalian bowers;
Remote from busy Life's bewilder'd way,
O'er all his heart shall Taste and Beauty sway;
Free on the sunny slope, or winding shore,
With hermit steps to wander and adore;
There shall he love, when genial morn appears,
Like pensive Beauty smiling in her tears,
To watch the bright'ning roses of the sky,
And muse on Nature with a poet's eye!
And when the sun's last splendour lights the deep,
The woods, and waves, and murmuring winds asleep;
When fairy harps th' Hesperian planets hail,
And the lone cuckoo sighs along the vale,

His path shall be where streamy mountains swell
Their shadowy grandeur o'er the narrow dell,
Where mouldering piles and forests intervene,
Mingling with darker tints the living green!
No circling hills his ravish'd eye to bound,
Heaven, earth, and ocean, blazing all around!

The moon is up—the watch-tower dimly burns—
And down the vale his sober step returns;
But pauses oft as winding rocks convey
The still sweet fall of Music far away!
And oft he lingers from his home awhile
To watch the dying notes!—and start, and smile!

Let Winter come! let polar spirits sweep
The darkening world, and tempest-troubled deep!
Though boundless snows the wither'd heath deform,
And the dim sun scarce wanders through the storm!
Yet shall the smile of social love repay,
With mental light, the melancholy day!
And, when its short and sullen noon is o'er,
The ice-chain'd waters slumbering on the shore,
How bright the fagots in his little hall
Blaze on the hearth, and warm the pictured wall!

How blest he names, in Love's familiar tone,
The kind fair friend, by nature mark'd his own!
And, in the waveless mirror of his mind,
Views the fleet years of pleasure left behind,

Since Anna's empire o'er his heart began!
Since first he call'd her his before the holy man!

Trim the gay taper in his rustic dome,
And light the wint'ry paradise of home!
And let the half-uncurtain'd window hail
Some way-worn man benighted in the vale!
Now, while the moaning night-wind rages high,
As sweep the shot-stars down the troubled sky,
While fiery hosts in Heaven's wide circle play,
And bathe in livid light the milky-way,
Safe from the storm, the meteor, and the shower,
Some pleasing page shall charm the solemn hour—
With pathos shall command, with wit beguile,
A generous tear of anguish, or a smile—
Thy woes, Arion! and thy simple tale, (*b*)
O'er all the heart shall triumph and prevail!
Charm'd as they read the verse too sadly true,
How gallant Albert, and his weary crew,
Heaved all their guns, their foundering bark to save,
And toil'd—and shriek'd—and perish'd on the wave!

Yes, at the dead of night, by Lonna's steep,
The seamen's cry was heard along the deep;
There on his funeral waters, dark and wild,
The dying father blest his darling child!
Oh! Mercy, shield her innocence, he cried,
Spent on the prayer his bursting heart, and died!

Or will they learn how generous worth sublimes
The robber Moor, (*c*) and pleads for all his crimes!
How poor Amelia kiss'd, with many a tear,
His hand blood-stain'd, but ever, ever dear!
Hung on the tortured bosom of her lord,
And wept, and pray'd perdition from his sword!
Nor sought in vain! at that heart-piercing cry
The strings of nature crack'd with agony!
He, with delirious laugh, the dagger hurl'd,
And burst the ties that bound him to the world!

Turn from his dying words, that smite with steel
The shuddering thoughts, or wind them on the wheel—
Turn to the gentler melodies that suit
Thalia's harp, or Pan's Arcadian lute;
Or, down the stream of Truth's historic page,
From clime to clime descend, from age to age!

Yet there, perhaps, may darker scenes obtrude
Than Fancy fashions in her wildest mood;
There shall he pause, with horrent brow, to rate
What millions died—that Cæsar might be great! (*d*)
Or learn the fate that bleeding thousands bore, (*e*)
March'd by their Charles to Dneiper's swampy shore,
Faint in his wounds, and shivering in the blast,
The Swedish soldier sunk—and groan'd his last!
File after file, the stormy showers benumb,
Freeze every standard-sheet, and hush the drum!

Horsemen and horse confess'd the bitter pang,
And arms and warriors fell with hollow clang!
Yet, ere he sunk in Nature's last repose,
Ere life's warm torrent to the fountain froze,
The dying man to Sweden turn'd his eye,
Thought of his home, and closed it with a sigh;
Imperial pride look'd sullen on his plight,
And Charles beheld—nor shudder'd at the sight!

Above, below, in Ocean, Earth, and sky,
Thy fairy worlds, Imagination, lie,
And Hope attends, companion of the way,
Thy dream by night, thy visions of the day!
In yonder pensile orb, and every sphere,
That gems the starry girdle of the year!
In those unmeasured worlds, she bids thee tell,
Pure from their God, created millions dwell,
Whose names and natures, unreveal'd below,
We yet shall learn, and wonder as we know;
For, as Iona's Saint, a giant form, (*f*)
Throned on her towers, conversing with the storm,
(When o'er each Runic altar, weed-entwined,
The vesper-clock tolls mournful to the wind,)
Counts every wave-worn isle, and mountain hoar
From Kilda to the green Ierne's shore;
So, when thy pure and renovated mind
This perishable dust hath left behind,
Thy seraph eye shall count the starry train,
Like distant isles embosom'd in the main;

Rapt to the shrine where motion first began,
And light and life in mingling torrent ran,
From whence each bright rotundity was hurl'd,
The throne of God,—the centre of the world!

Oh! vainly wise, the moral Muse hath sung
That suasive Hope hath but a Syren tongue!
True; she may sport with life's untutor'd day,
Nor heed the solace of its last decay,
The guileless heart her happy mansion spurn,
And part like Ajut—never to return! (*g*)

But yet, methinks, when Wisdom shall assuage
The griefs and passions of our greener age,
Though dull the close of life, and far away
Each flower that hail'd the dawning of the day;
Yet o'er her lovely hopes that once were dear,
The time-taught spirit, pensive, not severe,
With milder griefs her aged eye shall fill,
And weep their falsehood, though she love them still!

Thus, with forgiving tears, and reconciled,
The king of Judah mourn'd his rebel child!
Musing on days, when yet the guiltless boy
Smiled on his sire, and fill'd his heart with joy!
My Absalom! (the voice of nature cried!)
Oh! that for thee thy father could have died!
For bloody was the deed and rashly done,
That slew my Absalom!—my son!—my son!

Unfading Hope; when life's last embers burn,
When soul to soul, and dust to dust return!
Heaven to thy charge resigns the awful hour!
Oh! then, thy kingdom comes! Immortal Power!
What though each spark of earth-born rapture fly
The quivering lip, pale cheek, and closing eye
Bright to the soul thy seraph hands convey
The morning dream of life's eternal day—
Then, then, the triumph and the trance begin!
And all the Phœnix spirit burns within!

Oh! deep enchanting prelude to repose,
The dawn of bliss, the twilight of our woes!
Yet half I hear the parting spirit sigh,
It is a dread and awful thing to die!
Mysterious worlds, untravell'd by the sun!
Where Time's far-wandering tide has never run,
From your unfathom'd shades, and viewless spheres
A warning comes, unheard by other ears.
'T is Heaven's commanding trumpet, long and loud,
Like Sinai's thunder, pealing from the cloud!
While Nature hears, with terror-mingled trust,
The shock that hurls her fabric to the dust;
And, like the trembling Hebrew, when he trod
The roaring waves, and call'd upon his God,
With mortal terrors clouds immortal bliss,
And shrieks, and hovers o'er the dark abyss!

Daughter of Faith, awake, arise, illume
The dread unknown, the chaos of the tomb!

Melt, and dispel, ye spectre doubts, that roll
Cimmerian darkness on the parting soul!
Fly, like the moon-eyed herald of Dismay;
Chased on his night-steed by the star of day!
The strife is o'er—the pangs of Nature close,
And life's last rapture triumphs o'er her woes.
Hark! as the spirit eyes, with eagle gaze,
The noon of Heaven undazzled by the blaze,
On Heavenly winds that waft her to the sky,
Float the sweet tones of star-born melody;
Wild as that hallow'd anthem sent to hail
Bethlehem's shepherds in the lonely vale,
When Jordan hush'd his waves, and midnight still
Watch'd on the holy towers of Zion hill!

Soul of the just! companion of the dead!
Where is thy home, and whither art thou fled!
Back to its heavenly source thy being goes,
Swift as the comet wheels to whence he rose;
Doom'd on his airy path awhile to burn,
And doom'd, like thee, to travel and return.—
Hark! from the world's exploding centre driven,
With sounds that shook the firmament of Heaven,
Careers the fiery giant, fast and far,
On bick'ring wheels, and adamantine car;
From planet whirl'd to planet more remote,
He visits realms beyond the reach of thought;
But, wheeling homeward, when his course is run,
Curbs the red yoke, and mingles with the sun!

So hath the traveller of earth unfurl'd
Her trembling wings, emerging from the world;
And o'er the path by mortal never trod,
Sprung to her source, the bosom of her God!

Oh! lives there, Heaven! beneath thy dread ex
panse,
ne hopeless, dark Idolater of Chance,
Content to feed, with pleasures unrefined,
The lukewarm passions of a lowly mind;
Who, mould'ring earthward, 'reft of every trust,
In joyless union wedded to the dust,
Could all his parting energy dismiss,
And call this barren world sufficient bliss?—
There live, alas! of Heaven-directed mien,
Of cultured soul, and sapient eye serene,
Who hail'd thee, Man! the pilgrim of a day,
Spouse of the worm, and brother of the clay:
Frail as the leaf in Autumn's yellow bower,
Dust in the wind, or dew upon the flower!
A friendless slave, a child without a sire,
Whose mortal life, and momentary fire,
Lights to the grave his chance-created form
As ocean-wrecks illuminate the storm;
And when the gun's tremendous flash is o'er,
To Night and Silence sink for ever more!
Are these the pompous tidings ye proclaim,
Lights of the world, and demi-gods of Fame?
Is this your triumph—this your proud applause,
Children of Truth, and champions of her cause?

For this hath Science search'd on weary wing,
By shore and sea—each mute and living thing?
Launch'd with Iberia's pilot from the steep,
To worlds unknown, and isles beyond the deep?
Or round the cope her living chariot driven,
And wheel'd in triumph through the signs of Heaven?

Oh! star-eyed Science, hast thou wander'd there,
To waft us home the message of despair?
Then bind the palm, thy sage's brow to suit,
Of blasted leaf, and death-distilling fruit!
Ah me! the laurell'd wreath that murder rears,
Blood-nursed, and water'd by the widow's tears,
Seems not so foul, so tainted, and so dread,
As waves the night-shade round the sceptic head;
What is the bigot's torch, the tyrant's chain?
I smile on death, if Heaven-ward Hope remain!
But, if the warring winds of Nature's strife
Be all the faithless charter of my life,
If Chance awaked, inexorable power!
This frail and feverish being of an hour,
Doom'd o'er the world's precarious scene to sweep,
Swift as the tempest travels on the deep,
To know Delight but by her parting smile,
And toil, and wish, and weep a little while;
Then melt, ye elements, that form'd in vain
This troubled pulse, and visionary brain!
Fade, ye wild-flowers, memorials of my doom!
And sink, ye stars, that light me to the tomb!

Truth, ever lovely, since the world began,
The foe of tyrants, and the friend of man,—
How can thy words from balmy slumber start
Reposing Virtue, pillow'd on the heart!
Yet, if thy voice the note of thunder roll'd,
And that were true which Nature never told,
Let Wisdom smile not on her conquer'd field;
No rapture dawns, no pleasure is reveal'd!
Oh! let her read, nor loudly, nor elate,
The doom that bars us from a better fate;
But, sad as angels for the good man's sin,
Weep to record, and blush to give it in!

And well may Doubt, the mother of Dismay,
Pause at her martyr's tomb, and read the lay.
Down by the wilds of yon deserted vale,
It darkly hints a melancholy tale!
There, as the homeless madman sits alone,
In hollow winds he hears a spirit moan!
And there, they say, a wizard orgie crowds,
When the moon lights her watch-tower in the clouds.
Poor, lost Alonzo! Fate's neglected child!
Mild be the doom of Heaven—as thou wert mild!
For oh! thy heart in holy mould was cast,
And all thy deeds were blameless, but the last.
Poor, lost Alonzo! still I seem to hear
The clod that struck thy hollow-sounding bier!
When Friendship paid, in speechless sorrow drown'd,
Thy midnight rites, but not on hallow'd ground!

Cease every joy to glimmer on my mind,
But leave—oh! leave the light of Hope behind!
What though my winged hours of bliss have been,
Like angel-visits, few, and far between!
Her musing mood shall every pang appease,
And charm—when pleasures lose the power to please!

Yes! let each rapture, dear to Nature, flee;
Close not the light of Fortune's stormy sea—
Mirth, Music, Friendship, Love's propitious smile
Chase every care, and charm a little while,
Ecstatic throbs the fluttering heart employ,
And all her strings are harmonized to joy!—
But why so short is Love's delighted hour?
Why fades the dew on Beauty's sweetest flower?
Why can no hymned charm of Music heal
The sleepless woes impassion'd spirits feel?
Can Fancy's fairy hands no veil create,
To hide the sad realities of fate?—

No! not the quaint remark, the sapient rule,
Nor all the pride of Wisdom's worldly school,
Have power to soothe, unaided and alone,
The heart that vibrates to a feeling tone!
When step-dame Nature every bliss recalls,
Fleet as the meteor o'er the desert falls;
When, 'reft of all, yon widow'd sire appears
A lonely hermit in the vale of years;
Say, can the world one joyous thought bestow
To Friendship, weeping at the couch of Woe?

No! but a brighter soothes the last adieu,—
Souls of impassion'd mould, she speaks to you,
Weep not, she says, at Nature's transient pain,
Congenial spirits part to meet again!—

What plaintive sobs thy filial spirit drew,
What sorrow choked thy long and last adieu,
Daughter of Conrad! when he heard his knell,
And bade his country and his child farewell!
Doom'd the long isles of Sydney Cove to see,
The martyr of his crimes, but true to thee?
Thrice the sad father tore thee from his heart,
And thrice return'd, to bless thee and to part;
Thrice from his trembling lips he murmur'd low
The plaint that own'd unutterable woe;
Till Faith, prevailing o'er his sullen doom,
As burst the morn on night's unfathom'd gloom,
Lured his dim eye to deathless hopes sublime,
Beyond the realms of Nature and of time!

"And weep not thus, (he cried) young Ellenore,
My bosom bleeds, but soon shall bleed no more!
Short shall this half-extinguish'd spirit burn,
And soon these limbs to kindred dust return!
But not, my child, with life's precarious fire,
The immortal ties of Nature shall expire;
These shall resist the triumph of decay
When time is o'er, and worlds have pass'd away!
Cold in the dust this perish'd heart may lie,
But that which warm'd it once shall never die!

That spark unburied in its mortal frame,
With living light, eternal, and the same,
Shall beam on Joy's interminable years,
Unveil'd by darkness—unassuaged by tears!

"Yet on the barren shore and stormy deep,
One tedious watch is Conrad doom'd to weep;
But when I gain the home without a friend,
And press the uneasy couch where none attend,
This last embrace, still cherish'd in my heart,
Shall calm the struggling spirit ere it part!
Thy darling form shall seem to hover nigh,
And hush the groan of life's last agony!

"Farewell! when strangers lift thy father's bier,
And place my nameless stone without a tear;
When each returning pledge hath told my child
That Conrad's tomb is on the desert piled;
And when the dream of troubled fancy sees
Its lonely rank grass waving in the breeze;
Who then will soothe thy grief when mine is o'er?
Who will protect thee, helpless Ellenore?
Shall secret scenes thy filial sorrows hide,
Scorn'd by the world, to factious guilt allied?
Ah! no: methinks the generous and the good
Will woo thee from the shades of solitude!
O'er friendless grief compassion shall awake,
And smile on Innocence, for Mercy's sake!"

Inspiring thought of rapture yet to be,
The tears of love were hopeless, but for thee!
If in that frame no deathless spirit dwell,
If that faint murmur be the last farewell!
If fate unite the faithful but to part,
Why is their memory sacred to the heart?
Why does the brother of my childhood seem
Restored awhile in every pleasing dream?
Why do I joy the lonely spot to view,
By artless friendship bless'd when life was new?

Eternal Hope! when yonder spheres sublime
Peal'd their first notes to sound the march of Time,
Thy joyous youth began—but not to fade.—
When all the sister planets have decay'd;
When wrapt in fire the realms of ether glow,
And Heaven's last thunder shakes the world below;
Thou, undismay'd, shalt o'er the ruins smile,
And light thy torch at Nature's funeral pile!

NOTES

TO

PLEASURES OF HOPE.

PART II.

Note (*a*.) The noon of Manhood to a myrtle shade!

Sacred to Venus is the myrtle shade.——*Dryden.*

Note (*b*.) Thy woes, Arion!

Falconer, in his poem, *The Shipwreck*, speaks of himself by the name of Arion. See Falconer's *Shipwreck*, Canto III.

Note (*c*.) The robber Moor.

See Schiller's tragedy of the Robber, scene v.

Note (*d*.) What millions died that Cæsar might be great.

The carnage occasioned by the wars of Julius Cæsar has been usually estimated at two millions of men.

Note (*e*.) Or learn the fate that bleeding thousands bore,
March'd by their Charles to Dneiper's swampy shore.

In this extremity, (says the biographer of Charles XII. of Sweden, speaking of his military exploits before the battle of Pultowa,) the memorable winter of 1709, which was still more remarkable in that part of Europe than in France, destroyed numbers of his troops: for Charles resolved to brave the seasons as he had done his enemies, and ventured to make long marches during this mortal cold. It was in one of these marches that two thousand men fell down dead with cold, before his eyes.

Note (*f.*) As on Iona's height.

The natives of the island of Iona have an opinion, that on certain evenings every year, the tutelary saint Columba is seen on the top of the church spires, counting the surrounding islands, to see that they have not been sunk by the power of witchcraft.

Note (*g.*) And part, like Ajut,—never to return'

See the history of Ajut and Anningait, in the Rambler.

END OF PLEASURES OF HOPE.

ROGERS'S

PLEASURES OF MEMORY.

PART I.

Dolce sentier, ...
Colle, che mi piacesti, ...
Ov' ancor per usanza Amor mi mena;
Ben riconosco in voi l' usate forme, .
Non, lasso, in me, ...

ANALYSIS OF PART I.

The Poem begins with the description of an obscure village, and of the pleasing melancholy which it excites on being revisited after a long absence. This mixed sensation is an effect of the Memory. From an effect we naturally ascend to the cause; and the subject proposed, is then unfolded with an investigation of the nature and leading principles of this faculty.

It is evident that our ideas flow in continual succession, and introduce each other with a certain degree of regularity. They are sometimes excited by sensible objects, and sometimes by an internal operation of the mind. Of the former species is most probably the memory of brutes; and its many sources of pleasure to them, as well as to us, are considered in the first part. The latter is the most perfect degree of memory, and forms the subject of the second.

When ideas have any relation whatever, they are attractive of each other in the mind; and the perception of any object naturally leads to the idea of another, which was connected with it either in time or place, or which can be compared or contrasted with it. Hence arises our attachment to inanimate objects; hence also, in some degree, the love of our country, and the emotion with which we contemplate the celebrated scenes of antiquity. Hence a picture directs our thoughts to the original; and, as cold and darkness suggest forcibly the ideas of heat and light, he, who feels the infirmities of age, dwells most on whatever reminds him of the vigour and vivacity of his youth.

The associating principle, as here employed, is no less conducive to virtue than to happpiness; and, as such, it frequently discovers itself in the most tumultuous scenes of life. It addresses our finer feelings, and gives exercise to every mild and generous propensity.

Not confined to man, it extends through all animated nature; and its effects are peculiarly striking in the domestic tribes.

THE

PLEASURES OF MEMORY.

PART I.

Twilight's soft dews steal o'er the village-green,
With magic tints to harmonize the scene.
Still'd is the hum that through the hamlet broke,
When round the ruins of their ancient oak
The peasants flock'd to hear the minstrel play,
And games and carols closed the busy day.
Her wheel at rest, the matron thrills no more
With treasured tales, and legendary lore.
All, all are fled; nor mirth nor music flows
To chase the dreams of innocent repose.
All, all are fled; yet still I linger here!
What secret charms this silent spot endear!

Mark yon old Mansion frowning through the trees,
Whose hollow turret wooes the whistling breeze.
That casement arch'd with ivy's brownest shade,
First to these eyes the light of heaven convey'd.
The mouldering gateway strews the grass-grown court,
Once the calm scene of many a simple sport;
When nature pleased, for life itself was new,
And the heart promised what the fancy drew.

See, through the fractured pediment reveal'd,
Where moss inlays the rudely-sculptured shield,
The martin's old, hereditary nest:
Long may the ruin spare its hallow'd guest!

As jars the hinge, what sullen echoes call!
Oh haste, unfold the hospitable hall!
That hall, where once, in antiquated state,
The chair of justice held the grave debate.

Now stain'd with dews, with cobwebs darkly hung
Oft has its roof with peals of rapture rung;
When round yon ample board, in due degree,
We sweeten'd every meal with social glee.
The heart's light laugh pursued the circling jest;
And all was sunshine in each little breast.
'T was here we chased the slipper by the sound;
And turn'd the blindfold hero round and round.
'T was here, at eve, we form'd our fairy ring;
And Fancy flutter'd on her wildest wing.
Giants and genii chain'd each wondering ear;
And orphan-sorrows drew the ready tear.
Oft with the babes we wander'd in the wood,
Or view'd the forest-feats of Robin Hood:
Oft, fancy-led, at midnight's fearful hour,
With startling step we scaled the lonely tower;
O'er infant innocence to hang and weep,
Murder'd by ruffian hands, when smiling in its sleep.

Ye Household Deities! whose guardian eye
Mark'd each pure thought, ere register'd on high;
Still, still ye walk the consecrated ground,
And breathe the soul of Inspiration round.

As o'er the dusky furniture I bend,
Each chair awakes the feelings of a friend.
The storied arras, source of fond delight,
With old achievement charms the wilder'd sight;
And still, with Heraldry's rich hues imprest,
On the dim window glows the pictured crest.
The screen unfolds its many-colour'd chart,
The clock still points its moral to the heart.
That faithful monitor 't was heaven to hear,
When soft it spoke a promised pleasure near;
And has its sober hand, its simple chime,
Forgot to trace the feather'd feet of Time?
That massive beam, with curious carvings wrought,
Whence the caged linnet soothed my pensive thought;
Those muskets, cased with venerable rust;
Those once-loved forms, still breathing through their dust,
Still, from the frame in mould gigantic cast,
Starting to life—all whisper of the Past!

As through the garden's desert paths I rove,
What fond illusions swarm in every grove!

How oft, when purple evening tinged the west,
We watch'd the emmet to her grainy nest;
Welcomed the wild-bee home on weary wing,
Laden with sweets, the choicest of the spring!
How oft inscribed, with Friendship's votive rhyme,
The bark now silver'd by the touch of Time;
Soar'd in the swing, half pleased and half afraid,
Through sister elms that waved their summer-shade;
Or strew'd with crumbs yon root-inwoven seat,
To lure the redbreast from his lone retreat!

Childhood's loved group revisits every scene;
The tangled wood-walk, and the tufted green!
Indulgent MEMORY wakes, and lo, they live!
Clothed with far softer hues than Light can give.
Thou first, best friend that Heaven assigns below,
To soothe and sweeten all the cares we know;
Whose glad suggestions still each vain alarm,
When nature fades, and life forgets to charm;
Thee would the Muse invoke!—to thee belong
The sage's precept, and the poet's song.
What soften'd views thy magic glass reveals,
When o'er the landscape Time's meek twilight steals!
As when in ocean sinks the orb of day,
Long on the wave reflected lustres play;
Thy temper'd gleams of happiness resign'd,
Glance on the darken'd mirror of the mind.

The School's lone porch, with reverend mosses gray,
Just tells the pensive pilgrim where it lay.
Mute is the bell that rung at peep of dawn,
Quickening my truant-feet across the lawn:
Unheard the shout that rent the noontide air,
When the slow dial gave a pause to care.
Up springs, at every step, to claim a tear,
Some little friendship form'd and cherish'd here;
And not the lightest leaf, but trembling teems
With golden visions, and romantic dreams!

Down by yon hazel copse, at evening, blazed
The Gipsy's fagot—there we stood and gazed;
Gazed on her sun-burnt face with silent awe,
Her tatter'd mantle, and her hood of straw;
Her moving lips, her caldron brimming o'er;
The drowsy brood that on her back she bore,
Imps, in the barn with mousing owlet bred,
From rifled roost at nightly revel fed;
Whose dark eyes flash'd through locks of blackest shade,
When in the breeze the distant watch-dog bay'd:—
And heroes fled the Sibyl's mutter'd call,
Whose elfin prowess scaled the orchard-wall.
As o'er my palm the silver piece she drew,
And traced the line of life with searching view,
How throbb'd my fluttering pulse with hopes and fears,
To learn the colour of my future years!

Ah, then, what honest triumph flush'd my breast;
This truth once known—To bless is to be blest!
We led the bending beggar on his way,
(Bare were his feet, his tresses silver-gray,)
Soothed the keen pangs his aged spirit felt,
And on his tale with mute attention dwelt.
As in his scrip we dropt our little store,
And sigh'd to think that little was no more,
He breathed his prayer, "Long may such goodness live!"
'T was all he gave, 't was all he had to give.
Angels, when Mercy's mandate wing'd their flight,
Had stopt to dwell with pleasure on the sight.

But hark! through those old firs, with sullen swell,
The church-clock strikes! ye tender scenes, farewell!
It calls me hence, beneath their shade, to trace
The few fond lines that Time may soon efface.

On yon gray stone, that fronts the chancel-door,
Worn smooth by busy feet now seen no more,
Each eve we shot the marble through the ring,
When the heart danced, and life was in its spring;
Alas! unconscious of the kindred earth,
That faintly echo'd to the voice of mirth.

The glow-worm loves her emerald-light to shed,
Where now the sexton rests his hoary head.

Oft, as he turn'd the greensward with his spade,
He lectured every youth that round him play'd;
And calmly pointing where our fathers lay,
Roused us to rival each, the hero of his day.

Hush, ye fond flutterings, hush! while here alone
I search the records of each mouldering stone.
Guides of my life! Instructors of my youth!
Who first unveil'd the hallow'd form of Truth;
Whose every word enlighten'd and endear'd;
In age beloved, in poverty revered;
In Friendship's silent register ye live,
Nor ask the vain memorial Art can give.

But when the sons of peace, of pleasure sleep,
When only Sorrow wakes, and wakes to weep,
What spells entrance my visionary mind
With sighs so sweet, with transports so refined!

Ethereal Power! who at the noon of night
Recall'st the far-fled spirit of delight;
From whom that musing, melancholy mood
Which charms the wise, and elevates the good;
Blest MEMORY, hail! Oh grant the grateful Muse,
Her pencil dipt in Nature's living hues,
To pass the clouds that round thy empire roll,
And trace its airy precincts in the soul.

Lull'd in the countless chambers of the brain,
Our thoughts are link'd by many a hidden chain.

Awake but one, and lo, what myriads rise!*
Each stamps its image as the other flies.
Each, as the various avenues of sense
Delight or sorrow to the soul dispense,
Brightens or fades; yet all, with magic art,
Control the latent fibres of the heart.
As studious PROSPERO'S mysterious spell
Drew every subject-spirit to his cell;
Each, at thy call, advances or retires,
As judgment dictates, or the scene inspires.
Each thrills the seat of sense, that sacred source
Whence the fine nerves direct their mazy course,
And through the frame invisibly convey
The subtle, quick vibrations as they play;
Man's little universe at once o'ercast,
At once illumined when the cloud is past.

Survey the globe, each ruder realm explore;
From Reason's faintest ray to NEWTON soar.
What different spheres to human bliss assign'd!
What slow gradations in the scale of mind!
Yet mark in each these mystic wonders wrought;
Oh mark the sleepless energies of thought!

The adventurous boy, that asks his little share,
And hies from home with many a gossip's prayer,

---

* Namque illic posuit solium, et sua templa sacravit
Mens animi: hanc circum coëunt, densoque feruntur
Agmine notitiæ, simulacraque tenuia rerum.

Turns on the neighbouring hill, once more to see
The dear abode of peace and privacy;
And as he turns, the thatch among the trees,
The smoke's blue wreaths ascending with the breeze,
The village-common spotted white with sheep,
The church-yard yews round which his fathers sleep;
All rouse Reflection's sadly-pleasing train,
And oft he looks and weeps, and looks again.

So, when the mild Tupia dared explore
Arts yet untaught, and worlds unknown before,
And, with the sons of Science, woo'd the gale
That, rising, swell'd their strange expanse of sail;
So, when he breathed his firm yet fond adieu,
Borne from his leafy hut, his carved canoe,
And all his soul best loved—such tears he shed,
While each soft scene of summer-beauty fled.
Long o'er the wave a wistful look he cast,
Long watch'd the streaming signal from the mast;
Till twilight's dewy tints deceived his eye,
And fairy-forests fringed the evening-sky.

So Scotia's Queen, as slowly dawn'd the day,
Rose on her couch, and gazed her soul away.
Her eyes had bless'd the beacon's glimmering height,
That faintly tipt the feathery surge with light;
But now the morn with orient hues portray'd
Each castled cliff, and brown monastic shade:

All touch'd the talisman's resistless spring,
And lo, what busy tribes were instant on the wing!

Thus kindred objects kindred thoughts inspire,
As summer-clouds flash forth electric fire.
And hence this spot gives back the joys of youth,
Warm as the life, and with the mirror's truth.
Hence home-felt pleasure prompts the Patriot's sigh,
This makes him wish to live, and dare to die.
For this young Foscari, whose hapless fate
Venice should blush to hear the Muse relate,
When exile wore his blooming years away,
To sorrow's long soliloquies a prey,
When reason, justice, vainly urged his cause,
For this he roused her sanguinary laws;
Glad to return, though Hope could grant no more,
And chains and torture hail'd him to the shore.

And hence the charm historic scenes impart;
Hence Tiber awes, and Avon melts the heart.
Aërial forms in Tempe's classic vale,
Glance through the gloom, and whisper in the gale;
In wild Vaucluse with love and Laura dwell,
And watch and weep in Eloisa's cell.
'T was ever thus. Young Ammon, when he sought
Where Ilium stood, and where Pelides fought,
Sate at the helm himself. No meaner hand
Steer'd through the waves; and when he struck the land,

Such in his soul the ardour to explore,
PELIDES-like, he leap'd the first ashore.
'T was ever thus. As now at VIRGIL'S tomb
We bless the shade, and bid the verdure bloom:
So TULLY paused, amid the wrecks of Time,
On the rude stone to trace the truth sublime;
When at his feet, in honour'd dust disclosed,
The immortal Sage of Syracuse reposed.
And as he long in sweet delusion hung,
Where once a PLATO taught, a PINDAR sung;
Who now but meets him musing, when he roves
His ruin'd Tusculan's romantic groves!
In Rome's great forum, who but hears him roll
His moral thunders o'er the subject soul!

And hence that calm delight the portrait gives
We gaze on every feature till it lives!
Still the fond lover sees the absent maid;
And the lost friend still lingers in his shade!
Say why the pensive widow loves to weep,
When on her knee she rocks her babe to sleep:
Tremblingly still, she lifts his veil to trace
The father's features in his infant face.
The hoary grandsire smiles the hour away,
Won by the raptures of a game at play;
He bends to meet each artless burst of joy,
Forgets his age, and acts again the boy.

What though the iron school of War erase
Each milder virtue, and each softer grace;

What though the fiend's torpedo-touch arrest
Each gentler, finer impulse of the breast;
Still shall this active principle preside,
And wake the tear to Pity's self denied.
The intrepid Swiss, who guards a foreign shore,
Condemn'd to climb his mountain-cliffs no more,
If chance he hears the song so sweetly wild,
Which on those cliffs his infant hours beguiled,
Melts at the long-lost scenes that round him rise,
And sinks a martyr to repentant sighs.

Ask not if courts or camps dissolve the charm:
Say why VESPASIAN loved his Sabine farm;
Why great NAVARRE, when France and freedom bled,
Sought the lone limits of a forest-shed.
When DIOCLETIAN'S self-corrected mind
The imperial fasces of a world resign'd,
Say why we trace the labours of his spade,
In calm Salona's philosophic shade.
Say, when contentious CHARLES renounced a throne,
To muse with monks unletter'd and unknown,
What from his soul the parting tribute drew?
What claim'd the sorrows of a last adieu?
The still retreats that soothed his tranquil breast
Ere grandeur dazzled, and its cares oppress'd.

Undamp'd by time, the generous Instinct glows
Far as Angola's sands, as Zembla's snows;
Glows in the tiger's den, the serpent's nest,
On every form of varied life imprest.

The social tribes its choicest influence hail:—
And when the drum beats briskly in the gale,
The war-worn courser charges at the sound,
And with young vigour wheels the pasture round.

Oft has the aged tenant of the vale
Lean'd on his staff to lengthen out the tale;
Oft have his lips the grateful tribute breathed,
From sire to son with pious zeal bequeathed.
When o'er the blasted heath the day declined,
And on the scathed oak warr'd the winter-wind;
When not a distant taper's twinkling ray
Gleam'd o'er the furze to light him on his way;
When not a sheep-bell soothed his listening ear,
And the big rain-drops told the tempest near;
Then did his horse the homeward track descry,
The track that shunn'd his sad, inquiring eye;
And win each wavering purpose to relent,
With warmth so mild, so gently violent,
That his charm'd hand the careless rein resign'd,
And doubts and terrors vanish'd from his mind.

Recall the traveller, whose alter'd form
Has borne the buffet of the mountain-storm;
And who will first his fond impatience meet?
His faithful dog's already at his feet!
Yes, though the porter spurn him from the door,
Though all that knew him, know his face no more,
His faithful dog shall tell his joy to each,
With that mute eloquence which passes speech.—

And see, the master but returns to die!
Yet who shall bid the watchful servant fly?
The blasts of heaven, the drenching dews of earth,
The wanton insults of unfeeling mirth,
These, when to guard Misfortune's sacred grave,
Will firm Fidelity exult to brave.

Led by what chart, transports the timid dove
The wreaths of conquest, or the vows of love?
Say, through the clouds what compass points her flight?
Monarchs have gazed, and nations bless'd the sight.
Pile rocks on rocks, bid woods and mountains rise,
Eclipse her native shades, her native skies:—
'T is vain! through Ether's pathless wilds she goes,
And lights at last where all her cares repose.

Sweet bird! thy truth shall Harlem's walls attest,
And unborn ages consecrate thy nest.
When, with the silent energy of grief,
With looks that ask'd, yet dared not hope relief,
Want with her babes round generous Valour clung,
To wring the slow surrender from his tongue,
'T was thine to animate her closing eye;
Alas! 't was thine perchance the first to die,
Crush'd by her meagre hand, when welcomed from the sky.

Hark! the bee winds her small but mellow horn,
Blithe to salute the sunny smile of morn.

O'er thymy downs she bends her busy course,
And many a stream allures her to its source.
'T is noon, 't is night. That eye so finely wrought,
Beyond the search of sense, the soar of thought,
Now vainly asks the scenes she left behind;
Its orb so full, its vision so confined!
Who guides the patient pilgrim to her cell?
Who bids her soul with conscious triumph swell?
With conscious truth retrace the mazy clue
Of summer-scents, that charm'd her as she flew?
Hail MEMORY, hail! thy universal reign
Guards the least link of Being's glorious chain.

NOTES

TO

PLEASURES OF MEMORY.

PART I.

P. 66, l. 1.

How oft, when purple evening tinged the west.

VIRGIL, in one of his Eclogues, describes a romantic attachment as conceived in such circumstances; and the description is so true to nature, that we must surely be indebted for it to some early recollection. "You were little when I first saw you. You were with your mother gathering fruit in our orchard, and I was your guide. I was just entering my thirteenth year, and just able to reach the boughs from the ground."

So also Zappi, an Italian Poet of the last century. "When I used to measure myself with my goat, and my goat was the tallest, even then I loved Clori."

P. 67, l. 7.

Up springs, at every step, to claim a tear.

I came to the place of my birth, and cried, "The friends of my Youth, where are they?"—And an echo answered, "Where are they?"—*From an Arabic MS.*

P. 70, l. 1

Awake but one, and lo, what myriads rise!

When a traveller, who was surveying the ruins of Rome, expressed a desire to possess some relic of its ancient grandeur, Poussin, who attended him, stooped down, and gathering up a handful of earth shining with small grains of porphyry, "Take this home," said he, "for your cabinet; and say boldly, *Questa è Roma Antica.*"

P. 71, l. 6.

The church-yard yews round which his fathers sleep.

Every man, like Gulliver in Lilliput, is fastened to some spot of earth, by the thousand small threads which habit and association are continually stealing over him. Of these, perhaps, one of the strongest is here alluded to.

When the Canadian Indians were once solicited to emigrate, "What!" they replied, "shall we say to the bones of our fathers, Arise, and go with us into a foreign land?"

P. 71, l. 13.

So, when he breathed his firm yet fond adieu.

See Cook's first voyage, book i. chap. 16.

Another very affecting instance of local attachment is related of his fellow-countryman Potaveri, who came to Europe with M. de Bougainville.—See *Les Jardins, chant.* ii.

P. 71, l. 21.

So Scotia's Queen, &c.

Elle se leve sur son lict, et se met à contempler la France encore, et tant qu'elle peut.—*Brantôme.*

P. 72, l. 3.

Thus kindred objects kindred thoughts inspire.

To an accidental association may be ascribed some of the noblest efforts of human genius. The Historian of the Decline and Fall of the Roman Empire first conceived his design among the ruins of the Capitol; and to the tones of a Welsh harp are we indebted for the Bard of Gray.

P. 72, l. 7.

Hence home-felt pleasure, &c.

Who can enough admire the affectionate attachment of Plutarch, who thus concludes his enumeration of the advantages of a great city to men of letters? "As to myself, I live in a little town; and I choose to live there, lest it should become still less."—*Vit. Demosth.*

P. 72, l. 9.

For this young Foscari, &c.

He was suspected of murder, and at Venice suspicion was good evidence. Neither the interest of the Doge, his father, nor the intrepidity of conscious innocence, which he exhibited in the dungeon and on the rack, could procure his acquittal. He was banished to the island of Candia for life.

But here his resolution failed him. At such a distance from home he could not live; and, as it was a criminal offence to solicit the intercession of any foreign prince, in a fit of despair he addressed a letter to the Duke of Milan, and intrusted it to a wretch whose perfidy, he knew, would occasion his being remanded a prisoner to Venice.

P. 72, l. 17.

And hence the charm historic scenes impart.

Whatever withdraws us from the power of our senses; whatever makes the past, the distant, or the future, predominate over the present, advances us in the dignity of thinking beings. Far from me and from my friends be such frigid philosophy as may conduct us indifferent and unmoved over any ground which has been dignified by wisdom, bravery, or virtue. That man is little to be envied, whose patriotism would not gain force upon the plain of *Marathon*, or whose piety would not grow warmer among the ruins of *Iona.*—*Johnson.*

P. 72, l. 22.

And watch and weep in Eloisa's cell.

The Paraclete, founded by Abelard, in Champagne.

P. 72, l. 23.

'T was ever thus. Young Ammon, when he sought

Alexander, when he crossed the Hellespont, was in the twenty-second year of his age; and with what feelings must the Scholar of Aristotle have approached the ground described by Homer in that poem which had been his delight from his childhood, and which records the achievements of Him from whom he claimed his descent!

It was his fancy, if we may believe tradition, to take the tiller from Menœtius, and be himself the steersman during the passage. It was his fancy also to be the first to land, and to land full-armed.—*Arrian*, i. 11.

P. 73, l. 3.

As now at Virgil's tomb.

Vows and pilgrimages are not peculiar to the religious enthusiast. Silius Italicus performed annual ceremonies on the mountain of Posilipo; and it was there that Boccaccio, *quasi da un divino estro inspirato,* resolved to dedicate his life to the Muses.

P. 73, l. 5.

So Tully paused, amid the wrecks of time.

When Cicero was quæstor in Sicily, he discovered the tomb of Archimedes by its mathematical inscription. — *Tusc. Quæst.* v. 3.

P. 73, l. 19.

Say why the pensive widow loves to weep.

The influence of the associating principle is finely exemplified in the faithful Penelope, when she sheds tears over the bow of Ulysses.—*Od.* xxi. 55.

P. 74, l. 7.

If chance he hears the song so sweetly wild.

The celebrated Ranz des Vaches; cet air si chéri des Suisses qu'il fut défendu sous peine de mort de la jouer dans leurs troupes, parce qu'il faisoit fondre en larmes, déserter ou mourir ceux qui l'entendoient, tant il excitoit en eux l'ardent désir de revoir leur pays.—*Rousseau.*

The maladie de pays is as old as the human heart. JUVENAL's little cup-bearer

Suspirat longo non visam tempore matrem,
Et casulam, et notos tristis desiderat hœdos.

And the Argive, in the heat of battle,

Dulces moriens reminiscitur Argos,

P. 74, l. 12.

Say why Vespasian loved his Sabine farm.

This emperor, according to Suetonius, constantly passed the summer in a small villa near Reate, where he was born, and to which he would never add any embellishment; *ne quid scilicet oculorum consuetudini deperiret.*—*Suet. in Vit. Vesp.* cap. ii.

A similar instance occurs in the life of the venerable Pertinax, as related by J. Capitolinus. Posteaquam in Liguriam venit, multis agris coemptis, tabernam paternam, *manente formâ priore,* infinitis ædificiis circumdedit.—*Hist. August.* 54

And it is said of Cardinal Richelieu, that, when he built his magnificent palace on the site of the old family chateau at Richelieu, he sacrificed its symmetry to preserve the room in which he was born.—*Mém. de Mlle. de Montpensier,* i. 27.

An attachment of this nature is generally the characteristic of a benevolent mind; and a long acquaintance with the world cannot always extinguish it.

"To a friend," says John duke of Buckingham, "I will expose my weakness: I am oftener missing a pretty gallery in the old house I pulled down, than pleased with a saloon which I built in its stead, though a thousand times better in all respects."—See *his Letter to the D. of Sh.*

This is the language of the heart; and will remind the reader of that good-humoured remark in one of Pope's letters—"I should hardly care to have an old post pulled up, that I remembered ever since I was a child."

The Author of Telemachus has illustrated this subject with equal fancy and feeling, in the story of Alibée, Persan.

P. 74, l. 13.

Why great Navarre, &c.

That amiable and accomplished monarch, Henry the Fourth, of France, made an excursion from his camp, during the long siege of Laon, to dine at a house in the forest of Folambray; where he had often been regaled, when a boy, with fruit, milk, and new cheese; and in revisiting which he promised himself great pleasure.—*Mém de Sully.*

P. 74, l. 15.

When Diocletian's self-corrected mind.

Diocletian retired into his native province, and there amused himself with building, planting, and gardening. His answer to Maximian is deservedly celebrated. "If," said he, "I could show him the cabbages which I have planted with my own hands at Salona, he would no longer solicit me to return to a throne."

P. 74, l. 19.

Say, when contentious Charles, &c.

When the Emperor, Charles the Fifth had executed his memorable resolution, and had set out for the monastery of Justé, he stopt a few days at Ghent to indulge that tender and pleasant melancholy, which arises in the mind of every man in the decline of life, on visiting the place of his birth, and the objects familiar to him in his early youth.

P. 74, l. 20

To muse with monks, &c.

Monjes solitarios del glorioso padre San Geronimo, says Sandova.

In a corner of the Convent-garden there is this inscription. En esta santa casa de S. Geronimo de Justé se retiró à acabar u vida Cárlos V. Emperador, &c.—*Ponz.*

P. 75, l. 15.

Then did his horse the homeward track descry.

The memory of the horse forms the ground-work of a pleasing little romance entitled, " Lai du Palefroi vair."—See *Fabliaux du* XII. *Siecle.*

Ariosto likewise introduces it in a passage full of truth and nature. When Bayardo meets Angelica in the forest,

. . . Va mansueto a la Donzella,
. . . .
Ch'in Albracca il servia gia di sua mano.—*Orlando Furioso,* i. 75.

P. 76, l. 15.

Sweet bird! thy truth shall Harlem's walls attest.

During the siege of Harlem, when that city was reduced to the last extremity, and on the point of opening its gates to a base and barbarous enemy, a design was formed to relieve it; and the intelligence was conveyed to the citizens by a letter which was tied under the wing of a pigeon.—*Thuanus,* v. 5.

The same messenger was employed at the siege of Mutina, we are informed by the elder Pliny.—*Hist. Nat.* x. 37.

P. 76, l. 24.

Hark! the bee, &c.

This little animal, from the extreme convexity of her eye cannot see many inches before her.

ROGERS'S

PLEASURES OF MEMORY.

PART II

Delle cose custode e dispensiera.——*Tasso.*

ANALYSIS OF PART II.

The Memory has hitherto acted only in subservience to the senses, and so far man is not eminently distinguished from other animals: but, with respect to man, she has a higher province; and is often busily employed, when excited by no external cause whatever. She preserves, for his use, the treasures of art and science, history and philosophy. She colours all the prospects of life; for we can only anticipate the future, by concluding what is possible from what is past. On her agency depends every effusion of the Fancy, who with the boldest effort can only compound or transpose, augment or diminish the materials which she has collected.

When the first emotions of despair have subsided, and sorrow has softened into melancholy, she amuses with a retrospect of innocent pleasures, and inspires that noble confidence which results from the consciousness of having acted well. When sleep has suspended the organs of sense from their office, she not only supplies the mind with images, but assists in their combination. And even in madness itself, when the soul is resigned over to the tyranny of a distempered imagination, she revives past perceptions, and awakens that train of thought which was formerly most familiar.

Nor are we pleased only with a review of the brighter passages of life. Events, the most distressing in their immediate consequences, are often cherished in remembrance with a degree of enthusiasm

But the world and its occupations give a mechanical impulse to the passions, which is not very favourable to the indulgence of this feeling. It is in a calm and well-regulated mind that the Memory is most perfect; and solitude is her best sphere of action. With this sentiment is introduced a Tale illustrative of her influence in solitude, sickness, and sorrow. And the subject having now been considered, so far as it relates to man and the animal world, the Poem concludes with a conjecture that superior beings are blest with a nobler exercise of this faculty

THE

PLEASURES OF MEMORY.

PART II.

Sweet Memory, wafted by thy gentle gale,
Oft up the stream of Time I turn my sail,
To view the fairy haunts of long-lost hours,
Blest with far greener shades, far fresher flowers.

Ages and climes remote to Thee impart
What charms in Genius, and refines in Art;
Thee, in whose hand the keys of Science dwell,
The pensive portress of her holy cell;
Whose constant vigils chase the chilling damp
Oblivion steals upon her vestal-lamp.

They in their glorious course the guides of Youth,
Whose language breathed the eloquence of Truth;
Whose life, beyond preceptive wisdom, taught
The great in conduct, and the pure in thought;
These still exist, by Thee to Fame consign'd,
Still speak and act the models of mankind.

From thee gay Hope her airy colouring draws;
And Fancy's flights are subject to thy laws.

From thee that bosom-spring of rapture flows,
Which only Virtue, tranquil Virtue, knows.

When Joy's bright sun has shed his evening-ray,
And Hope's delusive meteors cease to play;
When clouds on clouds the smiling prospect close,
Still through the gloom thy star serenely glows;
Like yon fair orb, she gilds the brow of night
With the mild magic of reflected light.

The beauteous maid, who bids the world adieu,
Oft of that world will snatch a fond review;
Oft at the shrine neglect her beads, to trace
Some social scene, some dear, familiar face:
And ere, with iron tongue, the vesper-bell
Bursts through the cypress-walk, the convent-cell,
Oft will her warm and wayward heart revive,
To love and joy still tremblingly alive;
The whisper'd vow, the chaste caress prolong,
Weave the light dance, and swell the choral song;
With rapt ear drink the enchanting serenade,
And, as it melts along the moonlight-glade,
To each soft note return as soft a sigh,
And bless the youth that bids her slumbers fly.

But not till Time has calm'd the ruffled breast,
Are these fond dreams of happiness confest.
Not till the rushing winds forget to rave,
Is Heaven's sweet smile reflected on the wave.

From Guinea's coast pursue the lessening sail,
And catch the sounds that sadden every gale.
Tell, if thou canst, the sum of sorrows there;
Mark the fix'd gaze, the wild and frenzied glare,
The racks of thought, and freezings of despair!
But pause not then—beyond the western wave,
Go, see the captive barter'd as a slave!
Crush'd till his high, heroic spirit bleeds,
And from his nerveless frame indignantly recedes.

Yet here, even here, with pleasures long resign'd,
Lo! MEMORY bursts the twilight of the mind.
Her dear delusions soothe his sinking soul,
When the rude scourge assumes its base control;
And o'er Futurity's blank page diffuse
The full reflection of her vivid hues.
'T is but to die, and then, to weep no more,
Then will he wake on Congo's distant shore;
Beneath his plantain's ancient shade renew
The simple transports that with freedom flew;
Catch the cool breeze that musky Evening blows,
And quaff the palm's rich nectar as it glows;
The oral tale of elder time rehearse,
And chant the rude, traditionary verse
With those, the loved companions of his youth,
When life was luxury, and friendship truth.

Ah! why should Virtue fear the frowns of Fate?
Hers what no wealth can buy, no power create!

A little world of clear and cloudless day,
Nor wreck'd by storms, nor moulder'd by decay;
A world, with MEMORY'S ceaseless sun-shine blest,
The home of Happiness, an honest breast.

But most we mark the wonders of her reign,
When Sleep has lock'd the senses in her chain.
When sober Judgment has his throne resign'd,
She smiles away the chaos of the mind;
And, as warm Fancy's bright Elysium glows,
From her each image springs, each colour flows.
She is the sacred guest! the immortal friend!
Oft seen o'er sleeping Innocence to bend,
In that dead hour of night to Silence given,
Whispering seraphic visions of her heaven.

When the blithe son of Savoy, journeying round
With humble wares and pipe of merry sound,
From his green vale and shelter'd cabin hies,
And scales the Alps to visit foreign skies;
Though far below the forked lightnings play,
And at his feet the thunder dies away,
Oft, in the saddle rudely rock'd to sleep,
While his mule browses on the dizzy steep,
With MEMORY'S aid, he sits at home, and sees
His children sport beneath their native trees,
And bends to hear their cherub-voices call,
O'er the loud fury of the torrent's fall.

But can her smile with gloomy Madness dwell?
Say, can she chase the horrors of his cell?
Each fiery flight on Frenzy's wing restrain,
And mould the coinage of the fever'd brain?

Pass but that grate, which scarce a gleam supplies,
There in the dust the wreck of Genius lies!
He whose arresting hand divinely wrought
Each bold conception in the sphere of thought;
And round, in colours of the rainbow, threw
Forms ever fair, creations ever new!
But, as he fondly snatch'd the wreath of Fame,
The spectre Poverty unnerved his frame.
Cold was her grasp, a withering scowl she wore,
And Hope's soft energies were felt no more.
Yet still how sweet the soothings of his art!
From the rude wall what bright ideas start!
Even now he claims the amaranthine wreath,
With scenes that glow, with images that breathe!
And whence these scenes, these images, declare,
Whence but from Her who triumphs o'er despair?

Awake, arise! with grateful fervour fraught,
Go, spring the mine of elevating thought.
He, who, through Nature's various walks, surveys
The good and fair her faultless line portrays;
Whose mind, profaned by no unhallow'd guest,
Culls from the crowd the purest and the best;
May range, at will, bright Fancy's golden clime,
Or, musing, mount where Science sits sublime,
Or wake the spirit of departed Time.

Who acts thus wisely, mark the moral Muse,
A blooming Eden in his life reviews!
So rich the culture, though so small the space,
Its scanty limits he forgets to trace.
But the fond fool, when evening shades the sky,
Turns but to start, and gazes but to sigh!
The weary waste, that lengthen'd as he ran,
Fades to a blank, and dwindles to a span!

Ah! who can tell the triumphs of the mind,
By truth illumined, and by taste refined?
When age has quench'd the eye, and closed the ear,
Still nerved for action in her native sphere,
Oft will she rise—with searching glance pursue
Some long-loved image vanish'd from her view
Dart through the deep recesses of the past,
O'er dusky forms in chains of slumber cast;
With giant-grasp fling back the folds of night,
And snatch the faithless fugitive to light.
So through the grove the impatient mother flies,
Each sunless glade, each secret pathway tries;
Till the thin leaves the truant boy disclose,
Long on the wood-moss stretch'd in sweet repose.

Nor yet to pleasing objects are confined
The silent feasts of the reflecting mind.
Danger and death a dread delight inspire;
And the bald veteran glows with wonted fire,

When, richly bronzed by many a summer-sun,
He counts his scars, and tells what deeds were done.

Go, with old Thames, view Chelsea's glorious pile;
And ask the shatter'd hero, whence his smile?
Go, view the splendid domes of Greenwich—go,
And own what raptures from Reflection flow.

Hail, noblest structures imaged in the wave!
A nation's grateful tribute to the brave.
Hail, blest retreats from war and shipwreck, hail!
That oft arrest the wondering stranger's sail.
Long have ye heard the narratives of age,
The battle's havoc, and the tempest's rage;
Long have ye known Reflection's genial ray
Gild the calm close of Valour's various day.

Time's sombrous touches soon correct the piece,
Mellow each tint, and bid each discord cease:
A softer tone of light pervades the whole,
And steals a pensive languor o'er the soul.

Hast thou through Eden's wild-wood vales pursued
Each mountain-scene, majestically rude;
To note the sweet simplicity of life,
Far from the din of Folly's idle strife;
Nor there awhile, with lifted eye, revered
That modest stone which pious PEMBROKE rear'd;
Which still records, beyond the pencil's power,
The silent sorrows of a parting hour;

Still to the musing pilgrim points the place,
Her sainted spirit most delights to trace?

Thus, with the manly glow of honest pride,
O'er his dead son the gallant Ormond sigh'd.
Thus, through the gloom of Shenstone's fairy-grove,
Maria's urn still breathes the voice of love.

As the stern grandeur of a Gothic tower,
Awes us less deeply in its morning-hour,
Than when the shades of Time serenely fall
On every broken arch and ivied wall;
The tender images we love to trace,
Steal from each year a melancholy grace!
And as the sparks of social love expand,
As the heart opens in a foreign land;
And, with a brother's warmth, a brother's smile,
The stranger greets each native of his isle;
So scenes of life, when present and confess'd,
Stamp but their bolder features on the breast;
Yet not an image, when remotely view'd,
However trivial, and however rude,
But wins the heart, and wakes the social sigh,
With every claim of close affinity!

But these pure joys the world can never know;
In gentler climes their silver currents flow.
Oft at the silent, shadowy close of day,
When the hush'd grove has sung its parting lay;

When pensive Twilight, in her dusky car,
Comes slowly on to meet the evening-star;
Above, below, aërial murmurs swell,
From hanging wood, brown heath, and bushy dell!
A thousand nameless rills, that shun the light,
Stealing soft music on the ear of night.
So oft the finer movements of the soul,
That shun the sphere of Pleasure's gay control,
In the still shades of calm Seclusion rise,
And breathe their sweet, seraphic harmonies!

Once, and domestic annals tell the time,
(Preserved in Cumbria's rude, romantic clime)
When Nature smiled, and o'er the landscape threw
Her richest fragrance, and her brightest hue,
A blithe and blooming Forester explored
Those loftier scenes SALVATOR'S soul adored;
The rocky pass half-hung with shaggy wood,
And the cleft oak flung boldly o'er the flood;
Nor shunn'd the track, unknown to human tread,
That downward to the night of caverns led;
Some ancient cataract's deserted bed.

High on exulting wing the heath-cock rose,
And blew his shrill blast o'er perennial snows;
Ere the rapt youth, recoiling from the roar,
Gazed on the tumbling tide of dread Lodore;
And through the rifted cliffs, that scaled the sky,
Derwent's clear mirror charm'd his dazzled eye.

Each osier isle, inverted on the wave,
Through morn's gray mist its melting colours gave;
And, o'er the cygnet's haunt, the mantling grove
Its emerald arch with wild luxuriance wove.

Light as the breeze that brush'd the orient dew,
From rock to rock the young Adventurer flew;
And day's last sunshine slept along the shore,
When lo, a path the smile of welcome wore.
Embowering shrubs with verdure veil'd the sky,
And on the musk-rose shed a deeper dye;
Save when a bright and momentary gleam
Glanced from the white foam of some shelter'd stream.

O'er the still lake the bell of evening toll'd,
And on the moor the shepherd penn'd his fold;
And on the green hill's side the meteor play'd;
When, hark! a voice sung sweetly through the shade.
It ceased—yet still in FLORIO's fancy sung,
Still on each note his captive spirit hung;
Till o'er the mead, a cool, sequester'd grot
From its rich roof a sparry lustre shot.
A crystal water cross'd the pebbled floor,
And on the front these simple lines it bore.

Hence away, nor dare intrude!
In this secret, shadowy cell
Musing MEMORY loves to dwell,
With her sister Solitude.

Far from the busy world she flies,
To taste that peace the world denies.
Entranced she sits; from youth to age,
Reviewing Life's eventful page;
And noting, ere they fade away,
The little lines of yesterday.

FLORIO had gain'd a rude and rocky seat,
When lo, the Genius of this still retreat!
Fair was her form—but who can hope to trace
The pensive softness of her angel-face?
Can VIRGIL'S verse, can RAPHAEL'S touch impart
Those finer features of the feeling heart,
Those tenderer tints that shun the careless eye,
And in the world's contagious climate die?

She left the cave, nor mark'd the stranger there;
Her pastoral beauty, and her artless air
Had breathed a soft enchantment o'er his soul!
In every nerve he felt her blest control!
What pure and white-wing'd agents of the sky,
Who rule the springs of sacred sympathy,
Inform congenial spirits when they meet?
Sweet is their office, as their natures sweet!

FLORIO, with fearful joy, pursued the maid,
Till through a vista's moonlight-chequer'd shade,
Where the bat circled, and the rooks reposed,
(Their wars suspended, and their councils closed)

An antique mansion burst in awful state,
A rich vine clustering round the Gothic gate.
Nor paused he there. The master of the scene
Saw his light step imprint the dewy green;
And, slow-advancing, hail'd him as his guest,
Won by the honest warmth his looks express'd.
He wore the rustic manners of a Squire;
Age had not quench'd one spark of manly fire;
But giant Gout had bound him in her chain,
And his heart panted for the chase in vain.

Yet here Remembrance, sweetly-soothing Power!
Wing'd with delight Confinement's lingering hour.
The fox's brush still emulous to wear,
He scour'd the county in his elbow-chair;
And, with view-halloo, roused the dreaming hound,
That rung, by starts, his deep-toned music round.

Long by the paddock's humble pale confined,
His aged hunters coursed the viewless wind:
And each, with glowing energy portray'd,
The far-famed triumphs of the field display'd,
Usurp'd the canvas of the crowded hall,
And chased a line of heroes from the wall.
There slept the horn each jocund echo knew,
And many a smile and many a story drew!
High o'er the hearth his forest-trophies hung,
And their fantastic branches wildly flung.
How would he dwell on the vast antlers there!
These dash'd the wave, those fann'd the mountain-air,

All, as they frown'd, unwritten records bore
Of gallant feats and festivals of yore.

But why the tale prolong?—His only child,
His darling JULIA on the stranger smiled.
Her little arts a fretful sire to please,
Her gentle gaiety, and native ease
Had won his soul; and rapturous Fancy shed
Her golden lights, and tints of rosy red.
But ah! few days had pass'd, ere the bright vision
fled!

When Evening tinged the lake's ethereal blue,
And her deep shades irregularly threw;
Their shifting sail dropt gently from the cove,
Down by St. Herbert's consecrated grove;
Whence erst the chanted hymn, the taper'd rite
Amused the fisher's solitary night:
And still the mitred window, richly wreathed,
A sacred calm through the brown foliage breathed.

The wild deer, starting through the silent glade,
With fearful gaze their various course survey'd.
High hung in air the hoary goat reclined,
His streaming beard the sport of every wind;
And, while the coot her jet-wing loved to lave,
Rock'd on the bosom of the sleepless wave:
The eagle rush'd from Skiddaw's purple crest,
A cloud still brooding o'er her giant-nest.

And now the moon had dimm'd with dewy ray
The few fine flushes of departing day.
O'er the wide water's deep serene she hung,
And her broad lights on every mountain flung;
When lo, a sudden blast the vessel blew,
And to the surge consign'd the little crew.
All, all escaped—but ere the lover bore
His faint and faded JULIA to the shore,
Her sense had fled!—Exhausted by the storm,
A fatal trance hung o'er her pallid form;
Her closing eye a trembling lustre fired;
'T was life's last spark—it flutter'd and expired!

The father strew'd his white hairs in the wind,
Call'd on his child—nor linger'd long behind:
And FLORIO lived to see the willow wave,
With many an evening-whisper, o'er their grave.
Yes, FLORIO lived—and, still of each possess'd,
The father cherish'd, and the maid caress'd!

For ever would the fond enthusiast rove,
With JULIA's spirit, through the shadowy grove;
Gaze with delight on every scene she plann'd,
Kiss every floweret planted by her hand.
Ah! still he traced her steps along the glade,
When hazy hues and glimmering lights betray'd
Half-viewless forms; still listen'd as the breeze
Heaved its deep sobs among the aged trees;
And at each pause her melting accents caught,
In sweet delirium of romantic thought!

Dear was the grot that shunn'd the blaze of day;
She gave its spars to shoot a trembling ray.
The spring, that bubbled from its inmost cell,
Murmur'd of JULIA's virtues as it fell;
And o'er the dripping moss, the fretted stone,
In FLORIO's ear breathed language not its own.
Her charm around the enchantress MEMORY threw,
A charm that soothes the mind, and sweetens too!

But is her magic only felt below?
Say, through what brighter realms she bids it flow;
To what pure beings, in a nobler sphere,
She yields delight but faintly imaged here:
All that till now their rapt researches knew,
Not call'd in slow succession to review;
But, as a landscape meets the eye of day,
At once presented to their glad survey!

Each scene of bliss reveal'd, since chaos fled,
And dawning light its dazzling glories spread;
Each chain of wonders that sublimely glow'd,
Since first Creation's choral anthem flow'd;
Each ready flight, at Mercy's call divine,
To distant worlds that undiscover'd shine;
Full on her tablet flings its living rays,
And all, combined, with blest effulgence blaze.

There thy bright train, immortal Friendship, soar;
No more to part, to mingle tears no more!

And, as the softening hand of Time endears
The joys and sorrows of our infant years,
So there the soul, released from human strife,
Smiles at the little cares and ills of life;
Its lights and shades, its sunshine and its showers;
As at a dream that charm'd her vacant hours!

Oft may the spirits of the dead descend
To watch the silent slumbers of a friend;
To hover round his evening-walk unseen,
And hold sweet converse on the dusky green;
To hail the spot where once their friendship grew,
And heaven and nature open'd to their view!
Oft, when he trims his cheerful hearth, and sees
A smiling circle emulous to please;
There may these gentle guests delight to dwell,
And bless the scene they loved in life so well!

Oh thou! with whom my heart was wont to share
From Reason's dawn each pleasure and each care;
With whom, alas! I fondly hoped to know
The humble walks of happiness below;
If thy blest nature now unites above
An angel's pity with a brother's love,
Still o'er my life preserve thy mild control,
Correct my views, and elevate my soul;
Grant me thy peace and purity of mind,
Devout yet cheerful, active yet resign'd;
Grant me, like thee, whose heart knew no disguise,
Whose blameless wishes never aim'd to rise,

To meet the changes Time and Chance present,
With modest dignity and calm content.
When thy last breath, ere Nature sunk to rest,
Thy meek submission to thy God express'd;
When thy last look, ere thought and feeling fled,
A mingled gleam of hope and triumph shed;
What to thy soul its glad assurance gave,
Its hope in death, its triumph o'er the grave?
The sweet Remembrance of unblemish'd youth,
The still inspiring voice of Innocence and Truth!

Hail, MEMORY, hail! in thy exhaustless mine
From age to age unnumber'd treasures shine!
Thought and her shadowy brood thy call obey,
And Place and Time are subject to thy sway!
Thy pleasures most we feel, when most alone;
The only pleasures we can call our own.
Lighter than air, Hope's summer-visions die,
If but a fleeting cloud obscure the sky;
If but a beam of sober Reason play,
Lo, Fancy's fairy frost-work melts away!
But can the wiles of Art, the grasp of Power,
Snatch the rich relics of a well-spent hour?
These, when the trembling spirit wings her flight,
Pour round her path a stream of living light;
And gild those pure and perfect realms of rest,
Where Virtue triumphs, and her sons are blest!

NOTES

TO

PLEASURES OF MEMORY.

PART II.

P. 87, l. 15.

These still exist, &c.

THERE is a future Existence even in this world, an Existence in the hearts and minds of those who shall live after us. It is in reserve for every man, however obscure; and his portion, if he be diligent, must be equal to his desires. For in whose remembrance can we wish to hold a place, but such as know, and are known by us? These are within the sphere of our influence, and among these and their descendants we may live for evermore.

It is a state of rewards and punishments; and, like that revealed to us in the Gospel, has the happiest influence on our lives. The latter excites us to gain the favour of GOD, the former to gain the love and esteem of wise and good men; and both lead to the same end; for, in framing our conceptions of the DEITY, we only ascribe to Him exalted degrees of Wisdom and Goodness.

P. 91, l. 15.

Yet still how sweet the soothings of his art!

The astronomer chalking his figures on the wall, in Hogarth's view of Bedlam, is an admirable exemplification of this idea.—See *the Rake's Progress*, plate 8.

P. 92, l. 6.

Turns but to start, and gazes but to sigh!

The following stanzas are said to have been written on a blank leaf of this Poem. They present so affecting a reverse of the picture, that I cannot resist the opportunity of introducing them here.

Pleasures of Memory!—oh! supremely blest,
  And justly proud beyond a Poet's praise;
If the pure confines of thy tranquil breast
  Contain, indeed, the subject of thy lays!
    By me how envied!—for to me,
    The herald still of misery,
    Memory makes her influence known
    By sighs, and tears, and grief alone:
I greet her as the fiend, to whom belong
The vulture's ravening beak, the raven's funeral song.

She tells of time mispent, of comfort lost,
  Of fair occasions gone for ever by;
Of hopes too fondly nursed, too rudely cross'd.
  Of many a cause to wish, yet fear to die;
    For what, except the instinctive fear
    Lest she survive, detains me here,
    When "all the life of life" is fled?—
    What, but the deep inherent dread,
Lest she beyond the grave resume her reign,
And realize the hell that priests and beldames feign?

P. 93, l. 19.

Hast thou through Eden's wild-wood vales pursued.

On the road-side between Penrith and Appleby, there stands a small pillar with this inscription:

"This pillar was erected in the year 1656, by Ann Countess Dowager of Pembroke, &c. for a memorial of her last parting, in this place, with her good and pious mother, Margaret Countess Dowager of Cumberland, on the 2d of April, 1616; in memory whereof she hath left an annuity of 4*l.* to be distributed to the poor of the parish of Brougham, every

2d day of April for ever, upon the stone table placed hard by. Laus Deo!"

The Eden is the principal river of Cumberland, and rises in the wildest part of Westmoreland.

P. 94, l. 4.

O'er his dead son the gallant Ormond sigh'd.

"I would not exchange my dead son," said he, "for any living son in Christendom."—*Hume.*

The same sentiment is inscribed on an urn at the Leasowes. 'Heu, quanto minus est cum reliquis versari, quam tui meminisse!"

P. 99, l. 13.

Down by St. Herbert's consecrated grove;

A small island covered with trees, among which were formerly the ruins of a religious house.

P. 100, l. 5.

When lo! a sudden blast the vessel blew.

In a mountain-lake the agitations are often violent and momentary. The winds blow in gusts and eddies; and the water no sooner swells, than it subsides.—See *Bourn's Hist of Westmoreland.*

P. 101, l. 11.

To what pure beings, in a nobler sphere;

The several degrees of angels may probably have larger views, and some of them be endowed with capacities able to retain together, and constantly set before them, as in one picture, all their past knowledge at once.—*Locke.*

END OF PLEASURES OF MEMORY.

AKENSIDE'S

PLEASURES OF IMAGINATION.

A POEM IN THREE BOOKS

BOOK I.

Ασεβῦσμέν ἐςιν ἀνθρωπυ τὰς ϖαρὰ τῦ θευ χάρθας ἀτιμάζειν.

Epict. apud Arrian. II. 13.

ARGUMENT.

The subject proposed. Difficulty of treating it poetically The ideas of the Divine Mind, the origin of every quality pleasing to the imagination. The natural variety of constitution in the minds of men; with its final cause. The idea of a fine imagination, and the state of the mind in the enjoyment of those pleasures which it affords. All the primary pleasures of the imagination result from the perception of greatness, or wonderfulness, or beauty, in objects. The pleasure from greatness, with its final cause. Pleasure from novelty or wonderfulness, with its final cause. Pleasure from beauty, with its final cause. The connexion of beauty with truth and good, applied to the conduct of life. Invitation to the study of moral philosophy. The different degrees of beauty in different species of objects: colour; shape; natural concretes; vegetables; animals; the mind. The sublime the fair, the wonderful of the mind. The connexion of the imagination and the moral faculty. Conclusion.

THE

PLEASURES OF IMAGINATION.

BOOK I.

WITH what attractive charms this goodly frame
Of Nature touches the consenting hearts
Of mortal men ; and what the pleasing stores
Which beauteous imitation thence derives
To deck the poet's, or the painter's toil ;
My verse unfolds. Attend, ye gentle powers
Of musical delight ! and while I sing
Your gifts, your honours, dance around my strain.
Thou, smiling queen of every tuneful breast,
Indulgent Fancy ! from the fruitful banks
Of Avon, whence thy rosy fingers cull
Fresh flowers and dews to sprinkle on the turf
Where SHAKSPEARE lies, be present : and with thee
Let Fiction come, upon her vagrant wings
Wafting ten thousand colours through the air,
Which, by the glances of her magic eye,
She blends and shifts at will, through countless forms,
Her wild creation. Goddess of the lyre,
Which rules the accents of the moving sphere,
Wilt thou, eternal Harmony ! descend,

And join this festive train? for with thee comes
The guide, the guardian of their lovely sports,
Majestic Truth; and where Truth deigns to come,
Her sister Liberty will not be far.
Be present, all ye genii, who conduct
The wandering footsteps of the youthful bard,
New to your springs and shades: who touch his ear
With finer sounds: who heighten to his eye
The bloom of Nature; and before him turn
The gayest, happiest attitude of things.

Oft have the laws of each poetic strain
The critic-verse employ'd; yet still unsung
Lay this prime subject, though importing most
A poet's name: for fruitless is th' attempt,
By dull obedience and by creeping toil
Obscure to conquer the severe ascent
Of high Parnassus. Nature's kindling breath
Must fire the chosen genius; Nature's hand
Must string his nerves, and imp his eagle-wings,
Impatient of the painful steep, to soar
High as the summit; there to breathe at large
Ethereal air; with bards and sages old,
Immortal sons of praise. These flattering scenes,
To this neglected labour court my song;
Yet not unconscious what a doubtful task
To paint the finest features of the mind,
And to most subtle and mysterious things
Give colour, strength, and motion. But the love

Of Nature and the muses bids explore,
Through secret paths erewhile untrod by man,
The fair poetic region, to detect
Untasted springs, to drink inspiring draughts,
And shade my temples with unfading flowers
Cull'd from the laureate vale's profound recess,
Where never poet gain'd a wreath before.

From Heaven my strains begin; from Heaven descends
The flame of genius to the human breast,
And love and beauty, and poetic joy
And inspiration. Ere the radiant Sun
Sprang from the east, or 'mid the vault of night
The Moon suspended her serener lamp;
Ere mountains, woods, or streams, adorn'd the globe,
Or Wisdom taught the sons of men her lore;
Then lived th' Almighty One: then, deep retired
In his unfathom'd essence, view'd the forms,
The forms eternal of created things;
The radiant Sun, the Moon's nocturnal lamp,
The mountains, woods, and streams, the rolling globe,
And Wisdom's mien celestial. From the first
Of days, on them his love divine he fix'd,
His admiration: till in time complete,
What he admired and loved, his vital smile
Unfolded into being. Hence the breath
Of life informing each organic frame,
Hence the green earth, and wild resounding waves;

Hence light and shade alternate; warmth and cold;
And clear autumnal skies, and vernal showers,
And all the fair variety of things.

But not alike to every mortal eye
Is this great scene unveil'd. For since the claims
Of social life, to different labours urge
The active powers of man; with wise intent
The hand of Nature on peculiar minds
Imprints a different bias, and to each
Decrees its province in the common toil.
To some she taught the fabric of the sphere,
The changeful moon, the circuit of the stars,
The golden zones of Heaven; to some she gave
To weigh the moment of eternal things,
Of time, and space, and Fate's unbroken chain,
And Will's quick impulse: others by the hand
She led o'er vales and mountains, to explore
What healing virtue swells the tender veins
Of herbs and flowers; or what the beams of morn
Draw forth, distilling from the clefted rind
In balmy tears. But some to higher hopes
Were destined; some within a finer mould
She wrought, and temper'd with a purer flame.
To these the Sire Omnipotent unfolds
The world's harmonious volume, there to read
The transcript of himself. On every part
They trace the bright impressions of his hand:
In earth or air, the meadow's purple stores,

The Moon's mild radiance, or the virgin's form
Blooming with rosy smiles, they see portray'd
That uncreated beauty, which delights
The mind supreme. They also feel her charms,
Enamour'd; they partake the eternal joy.

For as old Memnon's image, long renown'd
By fabling Nilus, to the quivering touch
Of Titan's ray, with each repulsive string
Consenting, sounded through the warbling air
Unbidden strains; even so did Nature's hand
To certain species of external things,
Attune the finer organs of the mind:
So the glad impulse of congenial powers,
Or of sweet sounds, or fair-proportion'd form,
The grace of motion, or the bloom of light,
Thrills through Imagination's tender frame,
From nerve to nerve: all naked and alive,
They catch the spreading rays; till now the soul
At length discloses every tuneful spring,
To that harmonious movement from without
Responsive. Then the inexpressive strain
Diffuses its enchantment: Fancy dreams
Of sacred fountains and Elysian groves,
And vales of bliss: the intellectual power
Bends from his awful throne a wondering ear,
And smiles: the passions, gently soothed away,
Sink to divine repose, and love and joy
Alone are waking; love and joy serene

As airs that fan the summer. O! attend,
Whoe'er thou art, whom these delights can touch,
Whose candid bosom the refining love
Of Nature warms, O listen to my song;
And I will guide thee to her favourite walks,
And teach thy solitude her voice to hear,
And point her loveliest features to thy view.

Know then, whate'er of Nature's pregnant stores,
Whate'er of mimic Art's reflected forms
With love and admiration thus inflame
The powers of fancy, her delighted sons
To three illustrious orders have referr'd;
Three sister-graces, whom the painter's hand,
The poet's tongue, confesses; the sublime,
The wonderful, the fair. I see them dawn!
I see the radiant visions, where they rise,
More lovely than when Lucifer displays
His beaming forehead through the gates of morn,
To lead the train of Phœbus and the Spring.

Say, why was man so eminently raised
Amid the vast creation; why ordain'd
Through life and death to dart his piercing eye,
With thoughts beyond the limit of his frame;
But that the Omnipotent might send him forth
In sight of mortal and immortal powers,
As on a boundless theatre, to run
The great career of justice; to exalt

His generous aim to all diviner deeds;
To chase each partial purpose from his breast,
And through the mists of passion and of sense,
And through the tossing tide of chance and pain,
To hold his course unfaltering, while the voice
Of Truth and Virtue, up the steep ascent
Of Nature, calls him to his high reward,
The applauding smile of Heaven? Else wherefore burns
In mortal bosoms this unquenched hope,
That breathes from day to day sublimer things,
And mocks possession? wherefore darts the mind,
With such resistless ardour to embrace
Majestic forms; impatient to be free,
Spurning the gross control of wilful might;
Proud of the strong contention of her toils;
Proud to be daring? Who but rather turns
To Heaven's broad fire his unconstrained view,
Than to the glimmering of a waxen flame?
Who that, from Alpine heights, his labouring eye
Shoots round the wide horizon, to survey
Nilus or Ganges rolling his bright wave
Through mountains, plains, through empires black with shade,
And continents of sand; will turn his gaze
To mark the windings of a scanty rill
That murmurs at his feet? The high-born soul
Disdains to rest her heaven-aspiring wing
Beneath its native quarry. Tired of Earth

And this diurnal scene, she springs aloft
Through fields of air; pursues the flying storm;
Rides on the volley'd lightning through the heavens,
Or, yoked with whirlwinds, and the northern blast,
Sweeps the long tract of day. Then high she soars
The blue profound, and hovering round the Sun,
Beholds him pouring the redundant stream
Of light; beholds his unrelenting sway
Bend the reluctant planets to absolve
The fated rounds of Time. Thence far effused,
She darts her swiftness up the long career
Of devious comets; through its burning signs
Exulting measures the perennial wheel
Of Nature, and looks back on all the stars,
Whose blended light, as with a milky zone,
Invests the orient. Now amazed she views
The empyreal waste, where happy spirits hold,
Beyond this concave heaven, their calm abode;
And fields of radiance, whose unfading light
Has travell'd the profound six thousand years,
Nor yet arrives in sight of mortal things.
Even on the barriers of the world untired
She meditates the eternal depth below;
Till half recoiling, down the headlong steep
She plunges; soon o'erwhelm'd and swallow'd up
In that immense of being. There her hopes
Rest at the fated goal. For from the birth
Of mortal man, the sovereign Maker said,
That not in humble nor in brief delight,

Not in the fading echoes of Renown,
Power's purple robes, nor Pleasure's flowery lap,
The soul should find enjoyment: but from these
Turning disdainful to an equal good,
Through all the ascent of things enlarge her view,
Till every bound at length should disappear,
And infinite perfection close the scene.

Call now to mind what high capacious powers
Lie folded up in man; how far beyond
The praise of mortals, may the eternal growth
Of Nature to perfection half divine,
Expand the blooming soul? What pity then
Should sloth's unkindly fogs depress to Earth
Her tender blossom; choke the streams of life,
And blast her spring! Far otherwise design'd
Almighty Wisdom; Nature's happy cares
The obedient heart far otherwise incline.
Witness the sprightly joy when aught unknown
Strikes the quick sense, and wakes each active power
To brisker measures: witness the neglect
Of all familiar prospects, though beheld
With transport once; the fond attentive gaze
Of young astonishment; the sober zeal
Of age, commenting on prodigious things,
For such the bounteous Providence of Heaven,
In every breast implanting this desire
Of objects new, and strange, to urge us on
With unremitted labour to pursue

Those sacred stores that wait the ripening soul,
In Truth's exhaustless bosom. What need words
To paint its power? For this the daring youth
Breaks from his weeping mother's anxious arms,
In foreign climes to rove: the pensive sage,
Heedless of sleep, or midnight's harmful damp,
Hangs o'er the sickly taper; and untired
The virgin follows, with enchanted step,
The mazes of some wild and wondrous tale,
From morn to eve; unmindful of her form
Unmindful of the happy dress that stole
The wishes of the youth, when every maid
With envy pined. Hence, finally, by night
The village matron, round the blazing hearth,
Suspends the infant audience with her tales,
Breathing astonishment! of witching rhymes,
And evil spirits; of the death-bed call
Of him who robb'd the widow, and devour'd
The orphans' portion; of unquiet souls
Risen from the grave to ease the heavy guilt
Of deeds in life conceal'd; of shapes that walk
At dead of night, and clank their chains, and wave
The torch of Hell around the murderer's bed.
At every solemn pause the crowd recoil,
Gazing each other speechless, and congeal'd
With shivering sighs; till eager for the event,
Around the beldame all erect they hang,
Each trembling heart with grateful terrors quell'd.

But lo! disclosed in all her smiling pomp,
Where beauty onward moving claims the verse
Her charms inspire: the freely-flowing verse
In thy immortal praise, O form divine,
Smooths her mellifluent stream. Thee, Beauty, thee,
The regal dome, and thy enlivening ray
The mossy roofs adore: thou, better Sun!
For ever beamest on the enchanted heart
Love, and harmonious wonder, and delight
Poetic. Brightest progeny of Heaven!
How shall I trace thy features? where select
The roseate hues to emulate thy bloom?
Haste then, my song, through Nature's wide expanse,
Haste then, and gather all her comeliest wealth,
Whate'er bright spoils the florid earth contains,
Whate'er the waters, or the liquid air,
To deck thy lovely labour. Wilt thou fly
With laughing Autumn to the Atlantic isles,
And range with him the Hesperian field, and see
Where'er his fingers touch the fruitful grove,
The branches shoot with gold; where'er his step
Marks the glad soil, the tender clusters grow
With purple ripeness, and invest each hill
As with the blushes of an evening sky?
Or wilt thou rather stoop thy vagrant plume,
Where gliding through his daughter's honour'd shades,
The smooth Peneus from his glassy flood
Reflects purpureal Tempé's pleasant scene?

Fair Tempé! haunt beloved of sylvan powers,
Of Nymphs and Fauns; where in the golden age
They play'd in secret on the shady brink
With ancient Pan; while round their choral steps
Young Hours and genial Gales with constant hand
Shower'd blossoms, odours, shower'd embrosial dews,
And Spring's Elysian bloom. Her flowery store
To thee nor Tempé shall refuse; nor watch
Of winged Hydra guard Hesperian fruits
From thy free spoil. O bear then, unreproved,
Thy smiling treasures to the green recess
Where young Dione stays. With sweetest airs
Entice her forth to lend her angel-form
For Beauty's honour'd image. Hither turn
Thy graceful footsteps; hither, gentle maid,
Incline thy polish'd forehead: let thine eyes
Effuse the mildness of their azure dawn;
And may the fanning breezes waft aside
Thy radiant locks: disclosing, as it bends
With airy softness from the marble neck,
The cheek fair-blooming, and the rosy lip,
Where winning smiles and pleasures sweet as love,
With sanctity and wisdom, tempering blend
Their soft allurement. Then the pleasing force
Of Nature, and her kind parental care,
Worthier I'd sing: then all the enamour'd youth,
With each admiring virgin, to my lyre
Should throng attentive, while I point on high
Where Beauty's living image, like the morn

That wakes in Zephyr's arms the blushing May,
Moves onward; or as Venus, when she stood
Effulgent on the pearly car, and smiled,
Fresh from the deep, and conscious of her form,
To see the Tritons tune their vocal shells,
And each cerulean sister of the flood
With loud acclaim attend her o'er the waves,
To seek the Idalian bower. Ye smiling band
Of youths and virgins, who through all the maze
Of young desire with rival steps pursue
This charm of beauty; if the pleasing toil
Can yield a moment's respite, hither turn
Your favourable ear, and trust my words.
I do not mean to wake the gloomy form
Of Superstition dress'd in wisdom's garb,
To damp your tender hopes; I do not mean
To bid the jealous thunderer fire the heavens,
Or shapes infernal rend the groaning Earth
To fright you from your joys: my cheerful song
With better omens calls you to the field,
Pleased with your generous ardour in the chase,
And warm like you. Then tell me, for ye know,
Does Beauty ever deign to dwell where health
And active use are strangers? Is her charm
Confess'd in aught, whose most peculiar ends
Are lame and fruitless? Or did Nature mean
This pleasing call the herald of a lie;
To hide the shame of discord and disease,
And catch with fairy hypocrisy the heart

Of idle faith? O no: with better cares
The indulgent mother, conscious how infirm
Her offspring tread the paths of good and ill,
By this illustrious image, in each kind
Still most illustrious where the object holds
Its native powers most perfect, she by this
Illumes the headstrong impulse of desire,
And sanctifies his choice. The generous glebe
Whose bosom smiles with verdure, the clear tract
Of streams delicious to the thirsty soul,
The bloom of nectar'd fruitage ripe to sense,
And every charm of animated things,
Are only pledges of a state sincere,
The integrity and order of their frame,
When all is well within, and every end
Accomplish'd. Thus was Beauty sent from heaven,
The lovely ministress of truth and good
In this dark world: for truth and good are one,
And Beauty dwells in them, and they in her,
With like participation. Wherefore, then,
O sons of earth! would ye dissolve the tie?
O wherefore, with a rash impetuous aim,
Seek ye those flowery joys with which the hand
Of lavish Fancy paints each flattering scene
Where Beauty seems to dwell, nor once inquire
Where is the sanction of eternal truth,
Or where the seal of undeceitful good,
To save your search from folly! Wanting these,
Lo! Beauty withers in your void embrace,

And with the glittering of an idiot's toy
Did Fancy mock your vows. Nor let the gleam
Of youthful hope, that shines upon your hearts,
Be chill'd or clouded at this awful task,
To learn the lore of undeceitful good,
And truth eternal. Though the poisonous charms
Of baleful Superstition guide the feet
Of servile numbers through a dreary way
To their abode, through deserts, thorns, and mire;
And leave the wretched pilgrim all forlorn
To muse at last, amid the ghostly gloom
Of graves, and hoary vaults, and cloister'd cells;
To walk with spectres through the midnight shade,
And to the screaming owl's accursed song
Attune the dreadful workings of his heart;
Yet be not ye dismay'd. A gentler star
Your lovely search illumines. From the grove
Where Wisdom talk'd with her Athenian sons,
Could my ambitious hand entwine a wreath
Of Plato's olive with the Mantuan bay,
Then should my powerful verse at once dispel
Those monkish horrors: then in light divine
Disclose the Elysian prospect, where the steps
Of those whom Nature charms, through blooming walks,
Through fragrant mountains and poetic streams,
Amid the train of sages, heroes, bards,
Led by their winged Genius and the choir
Of laurel'd Science, and harmonious Art,

Proceed, exulting, to the eternal shrine,
Where Truth conspicuous with her sister-twins,
The undivided partners of her sway,
With Good and Beauty reigns. O let not us,
Lull'd by luxurious Pleasure's languid strain,
Or crouching to the frowns of Bigot rage,
O let us not a moment pause to join
That godlike band. And if the gracious Power
Who first awaken'd my untutor'd song,
Will to my invocation breathe anew
The tuneful spirit; then through all our paths,
Ne'er shall the sound of this devoted lyre
Be wanting; whether on the rosy mead,
When summer smiles, to warm the melting heart
Of Luxury's allurement; whether firm
Against the torrent and the stubborn hill
To urge bold Virtue's unremitted nerve,
And wake the strong divinity of soul
That conquers Chance and Fate; or whether struck
For sounds of triumph, to proclaim her toils
Upon the lofty summit, round her brow
To twine the wreath of incorruptive praise;
To trace her hallow'd light through future worlds,
And bless Heaven's image in the heart of man.

Thus with a faithful aim have we presumed,
Adventurous, to delineate Nature's form;
Whether in vast, majestic pomp array'd,
Or drest for pleasing wonder, or serene

In Beauty's rosy smile. It now remains,
Through various being's fair-proportion'd scale,
To trace the rising lustre of her charms,
From their first twilight, shining forth at length
To full meridian splendour. Of degree
The least and lowliest, in the effusive warmth
Of colours mingling with a random blaze,
Doth beauty dwell. Then higher in the line
And variation of determined shape,
Where Truth's eternal measures mark the bound
Of circle, cube, or sphere. The third ascent
Unites this varied symmetry of parts
With colour's bland allurement; as the pearl
Shines in the concave of its azure bed,
And painted shells indent their speckled wreath.
Then more attractive rise the blooming forms,
Through which the breath of Nature has infused
Her genial power to draw with pregnant veins
Nutritious moisture from the bounteous Earth,
In fruit and seed prolific: thus the flowers
Their purple honours with the spring resume;
And thus the stately tree with Autumn bends
With blushing treasures. But more lovely still
Is Nature's charm, where to the full consent
Of complicated members to the bloom
Of colour, and the vital change of growth,
Life's holy flame and piercing sense are given,
And active motion speaks the temper'd soul:
So moves the bird of Juno; so the steed

With rival ardour beats the dusty plain,
And faithful dogs, with eager airs of joy,
Salute their fellows. Thus doth Beauty dwell
There most conspicuous, even in outward shape,
Where dawns the high expression of a mind:
By steps conducting our enraptured search
To that eternal origin, whose power,
Through all the unbounded symmetry of things,
Like rays effulging from the parent Sun,
This endless mixture of her charms diffused.
Mind, mind alone, (bear witness, Earth and Heaven!)
The living fountains in itself contains
Of beauteous and sublime: here, hand in hand,
Sit paramount the Graces; here enthroned,
Celestial Venus, with divinest airs,
Invites the soul to never-fading joy.
Look then abroad through Nature, to the range
Of planets, suns, and adamantine spheres,
Wheeling unshaken through the void immense;
And speak, O man! does this capacious scene
With half that kindling majesty dilate
The strong conception, as when Brutus rose
Refulgent from the stroke of Cæsar's fate,
Amid the crowd of patriots; and his arm
Aloft extending, like eternal Jove,
When guilt brings down the thunder, call'd aloud
On Tully's name, and shook his crimson steel,
And bade the father of his country hail?
For lo! the tyrant prostrate on the dust,

And Rome again is free! is aught so fair
In all the dewy landscapes of the Spring,
In the bright eye of Hesper or the Morn,
In Nature's fairest forms, is aught so fair
As virtuous Friendship? as the candid blush
Of him who strives with fortune to be just?
The graceful tear that streams for others' woes?
Or the mild majesty of private life,
Where Peace with ever-blooming olive crowns
The gate; where Honour's liberal hands effuse
Unenvied treasures, and the snowy wings
Of Innocence and Love protect the scene?
Once more search, undismay'd, the dark profound
Where Nature works in secret; view the beds
Of mineral treasure, and the eternal vault
That bounds the hoary Ocean; trace the forms
Of atoms moving with incessant change
Their elemental round; behold the seeds
Of being, and the energy of life,
Kindling the mass with ever-active flame:
Then to the secrets of the working mind
Attentive turn; from dim oblivion call
Her fleet, ideal band; and bid them, go!
Break through Time's barrier, and o'ertake the hour
That saw the heavens created: then declare
If aught were found in those external scenes
To move thy wonder now. For what are all
The forms which brute, unconscious matter wears,
Greatness of bulk, or symmetry of parts?

Not reaching to the heart, soon feeble grows
The superficial impulse; dull their charms,
And satiate soon, and pall the languid eye.
Not so the moral species, nor the powers
Of genius and design; the ambitious mind
There sees herself: by these congenial forms
Touch'd and awaken'd, with intenser act
She bends each nerve, and meditates well-pleased
Her features in the mirror. For of all
The inhabitants of Earth, to man alone
Creative Wisdom gave to lift his eye
To Truth's eternal measures; thence to frame
The sacred laws of action and of will,
Discerning justice from unequal deeds,
And temperance from folly. But beyond
This energy of Truth, whose dictates bind
Assenting reason, the benignant sire,
To deck the honour'd paths of just and good,
Has added bright Imagination's rays:
Where Virtue, rising from the awful depth
Of Truth's mysterious bosom, doth forsake
The unadorn'd condition of her birth;
And, dress'd by Fancy in ten thousand hues,
Assumes a various feature, to attract,
With charms responsive to each gazer's eye,
The hearts of men. Amid his rural walk,
The ingenuous youth, whom solitude inspires
With purest wishes, from the pensive shade
Beholds her moving, like a virgin-muse

That wakes her lyre to some indulgent theme
Of harmony and wonder: while among
The herd of servile minds her strenuous form
Indignant flashes on the patriot's eye,
And through the rolls of memory appeals
To ancient honour, or, in act serene,
Yet watchful, raises the majestic sword
Of public power, from dark ambition's reach
To guard the sacred volume of the laws.

Genius of ancient Greece! whose faithful steps
Well-pleased I follow through the sacred paths
Of Nature and of Science; nurse divine
Of all heroic deeds and fair desires!
O! let the breath of thy extended praise
Inspire my kindling bosom to the height
Of this untempted theme. Nor be my thoughts
Presumptuous counted, if amid the calm
That soothes this vernal evening into smiles,
I steal impatient from the sordid haunts
Of Strife and low Ambition, to attend
Thy sacred presence in the sylvan shade,
By their malignant footsteps ne'er profaned.
Descend, propitious! to my favour'd eye;
Such in thy mien, thy warm, exalted air,
As when the Persian tyrant, foil'd and stung
With shame and desperation, gnash'd his teeth
To see thee rend the pageants of his throne;
And at the lightning of thy lifted spear

Crouch'd like a slave. Bring all thy martial spoils,
Thy palms, thy laurels, thy triumphal songs,
Thy smiling band of arts, thy godlike sires
Of civil wisdom, thy heroic youth
Warm from the schools of glory. Guide my way
Through fair Lycéum's walk, the green retreats
Of Academus, and the thymy vale,
Where, oft enchanted with Socratic sounds,
Ilissus pure devolved his tuneful stream
In gentler murmurs. From the blooming store
Of these auspicious fields, may I unblamed
Transplant some living blossoms to adorn
My native clime: while far above the flight
Of Fancy's plume aspiring, I unlock
The springs of ancient Wisdom! while I join
Thy name, thrice-honour'd! with the immortal praise
Of Nature, while to my compatriot youth
I point the high example of thy sons,
And tune to Attic themes the British lyre.

AKENSIDE'S

PLEASURES OF IMAGINATION.

BOOK II.

ARGUMENT.

The separation of the works of imagination from philosophy, the cause of their abuse among the moderns. Prospect of their reunion under the influence of public liberty. Enumeration of accidental pleasures, which increase the effect of objects delightful to the imagination. The pleasures of sense. Particular circumstances of the mind. Discovery of truth. Perception of contrivance and design. Emotion of the passions. All the natural passions partake of a pleasing sensation; with the final cause of this constitution illustrated by an allegorical vision, and exemplified in sorrow, pity, terror, and indignation

THE

PLEASURES OF IMAGINATION.

BOOK II.

When shall the laurel and the vocal string
Resume their honours? When shall we behold
The tuneful tongue, the Promethean hand,
Aspire to ancient praise? Alas! how faint,
How slow, the dawn of Beauty and of Truth
Breaks the reluctant shades of Gothic night,
Which yet involve the nations! Long they groan'd
Beneath the furies of rapacious Force;
Oft as the gloomy North, with iron swarms
Tempestuous pouring from her frozen caves,
Blasted the Italian shore, and swept the works
Of Liberty and Wisdom down the gulf
Of all-devouring night. As long immured
In noontide darkness by the glimmering lamp,
Each Muse and each fair Science pined away
The sordid hours: while foul, barbarian hands
Their mysteries profaned, unstrung the lyre,
And chain'd the soaring pinion down to Earth.
At last the Muses rose, and spurn'd their bounds,
And, wildly warbling scatter'd, as they flew,

Their blooming wreaths from fair Valclusa's bowers
To Arno's myrtle border, and the shore
Of soft Parthenope. But still the rage
Of dire Ambition and gigantic Power,
From public aims and from the busy walk
Of civil Commerce, drove the bolder train
Of penetrating Science to the cells,
Where studious Ease consumes the silent hour
In shadowy searches and unfruitful care.
Thus from their guardians torn, the tender arts
Of mimic Fancy, and harmonious Joy,
To priestly domination and the lust
Of lawless courts, their amiable toil
For three inglorious ages have resign'd,
In vain reluctant: and Torquato's tongue
Was tuned for slavish pæans at the throne
Of tinsel pomp: and RAPHAEL'S magic hand
Effused its fair creation to enchant
The fond adoring herd in Latian fanes
To blind belief; while on their prostrate necks
The sable tyrant plants his heel secure.
But now, behold! the radiant era dawns,
When Freedom's ample fabric, fix'd at length
For endless years on Albion's happy shore
In full proportion, once more shall extend
To all the kindred powers of social bliss,
A common mansion, a parental roof.
There shall the Virtues, there shall Wisdom's train,
Their long-lost friends rejoining, as of old,

Embrace the smiling family of Arts,
The Muses and the Graces. Then no more
Shall Vice, distracting their delicious gifts
To aims abhorr'd, with high distaste and scorn
Turn from their charms the philosophic eye,
The patriot-bosom; then no more the paths
Of public care or intellectual toil,
Alone by footsteps haughty and severe
In gloomy state be trod: the harmonious Muse,
And her persuasive sisters, then shall plant
Their sheltering laurels o'er the black ascent,
And scatter flowers along the rugged way.
Arm'd with the lyre, already have we dared
To pierce divine Philosophy's retreats,
And teach the Muse her lore; already strove
Their long-divided honours to unite,
While tempering this deep argument we sang
Of Truth and Beauty. Now the same glad task
Impends; now urging our ambitious toil,
We hasten to recount the various springs
Of adventitious pleasure which adjoin
Their grateful influence to the prime effect
Of objects grand or beauteous, and enlarge
The complicated joy. The sweets of sense,
Do they not oft with kind accession flow,
To raise harmonious Fancy's native charm?
So while we taste the fragrance of the rose,
Glows not her blush the fairer? While we view
Amid the noontide walk a limpid rill

Gush through the trickling herbage, to the thirst
Of Summer yielding the delicious draught
Of cool refreshment; o'er the mossy brink
Shines not the surface clearer, and the waves
With sweeter music murmur as they flow?

Nor this alone; the various lot of life
Oft from external circumstance assumes
A moment's disposition to rejoice
In those delights which at a different hour
Would pass unheeded. Fair the face of Spring
When rural songs and odours wake the Morn,
To every eye; but how much more to his
Round whom the bed of sickness long diffused
Its melancholy gloom! how doubly fair,
When first with fresh-born vigour he inhales
The balmy breeze, and feels the blessed Sun
Warm at his bosom, from the springs of life
Chasing oppressive damps and languid pain!

Or shall I mention, where celestial Truth
Her awful light discloses, to bestow
A more majestic pomp on Beauty's frame?
For man loves knowledge, and the beams of Truth
More welcome touch his understanding's eye,
Than all the blandishments of sound his ear,
Than all of taste his tongue. Nor ever yet
The melting rainbow's vernal-tinctured hues
To me have shone so pleasing, as when first

The hand of Science pointed out the path
In which the sunbeams gleaming from the west
Fall on the watery cloud, whose darksome veil
Involves the orient; and that trickling shower
Piercing through every crystalline convex
Of clustering dew-drops to their flight opposed,
Recoil at length where concave all behind
The internal surface on each glassy orb
Repels their forward passage into air;
That thence direct they seek the radiant goal
From which their course began; and, as they strike
In different lines, the gazer's obvious eye,
Assume a different lustre, through the brede
Of colours changing from the splendid rose,
To the pale violet's dejected hue.

Or shall we touch that kind access of joy,
That springs to each fair object, while we trace
Through all its fabric, Wisdom's artful aim
Disposing every part, and gaining still
By means proportion'd her benignant end?
Speak, ye, the pure delight, whose favour'd steps
The lamp of Science through the jealous maze
Of Nature guides, when haply you reveal
Her secret honours: whether in the sky,
The beauteous laws of light, the central powers
That wheel the pensile planets round the year;
Whether in wonders of the rolling deep,
Or the rich fruits of all-sustaining earth,

Or fine-adjusted springs of life and sense,
Ye scan the counsels of their author's hand.

What, when to raise the meditated scene,
The flame of passion through the struggling soul
Deep-kindled, shows across that sudden blaze
The object of its rapture, vast of size,
With fiercer colours and a night of shade?
What? like a storm from their capacious bed
The sounding seas o'erwhelming, when the might
Of these eruptions, working from the depth
Of man's strong apprehension, shakes his frame
Even to the base; from every naked sense
Of pain or pleasure dissipating all
Opinion's feeble coverings, and the veil
Spun from the cobweb fashion of the times
To hide the feeling heart? Then Nature speaks
Her genuine language, and the words of men,
Big with the very motion of their souls,
Declare with what accumulated force
The impetuous nerve of passion urges on
The native weight and energy of things.

Yet more: her honours where nor beauty claims
Nor shows of good the thirsty sense allure,
From Passion's power alone our nature holds
Essential pleasure. Passion's fierce illapse
Rouses the mind's whole fabric; with supplies
Of daily impulse keeps the elastic powers

Intensely poised, and polishes anew
By that collision all the fine machine:
Else rust would rise, and foulness, by degrees
Encumbering, choke at last what Heaven design'd
For ceaseless motion and a round of toil.
—But say, does every passion thus to man
Administer delight? That name indeed
Becomes the rosy breath of Love; becomes
The radiant smiles of Joy, the applauding hand
Of Admiration: but the bitter shower
That Sorrow sheds upon a brother's grave,
But the dumb palsy of nocturnal Fear,
Or those consuming fires that gnaw the heart
Of panting Indignation, find we there
To move delight?—Then listen while my tongue
The unalter'd will of Heaven with faithful awe
Reveals; what old Harmodius, wont to teach
My early age; Harmodius, who had weigh'd
Within his learned mind whate'er the schools
Of Wisdom, or thy lonely-whispering voice,
O faithful Nature! dictate of the laws
Which govern and support this mighty frame
Of universal being. Oft the hours
From morn to eve have stolen unmark'd away,
While mute attention hung upon his lips,
As thus the sage his awful tale began.

"'T was in the windings of an ancient wood,
When spotless youth with solitude resigns

To sweet philosophy the studious day,
What time pale Autumn shades the silent eve,
Musing I roved. Of good and evil much,
And much of mortal man, my thoughts revolved;
When starting full on Fancy's gushing eye
The mournful image of Parthenia's fate,
That hour, O long beloved and long deplored!
When blooming youth, nor gentlest Wisdom's arts,
Nor Hymen's honours gather'd for thy brow,
Nor all thy lover's, all thy father's tears,
Avail'd to snatch thee from the cruel grave;
Thy agonizing looks, thy last farewell,
Struck to the inmost feeling of my soul
As with the hand of Death. At once the shade
More horrid nodded o'er me, and the winds
With hoarser murmuring shook the branches. Dark
As midnight storms, the scene of human things
Appear'd before me: deserts, burning sands,
Where the parch'd adder dies; the frozen south,
And Desolation blasting all the west
With rapine and with murder: tyrant Power
Here sits enthroned with blood; the baleful charms
Of Superstition there infect the skies,
And turn the Sun to horror. Gracious Heaven!
What is the life of man? Or cannot these,
Not these portents thy awful will suffice?
That, propagated thus beyond their scope,
They rise to act their cruelties anew
In my afflicted bosom, thus decreed

The universal sensitive of pain,
The wretched heir of evils not its own!

"Thus I impatient; when at once effused,
A flashing torrent of celestial day
Burst through the shadowy void. With slow descent
A purple cloud came floating through the sky,
And, poised at length within the circling trees,
Hung obvious to my view; till opening wide
Its lucid orb, a more than human form
Emerging lean'd majestic o'er my head,
And instant thunder shook the conscious grove.
Then melted into air the liquid cloud,
Then all the shining vision stood reveal'd.
A wreath of palm his ample forehead bound,
And o'er his shoulder, mantling to his knee,
Flow'd the transparent robe, around his waist
Collected with a radiant zone of gold
Ethereal: there in mystic signs engraved,
I read his office high, and sacred name,
Genius of human-kind. Appall'd I gazed
The godlike presence; for athwart nis brow
Displeasure, temper'd with a mild concern,
Look'd down reluctant on me, and his words
Like distant thunders broke the murmuring air.

"'Vain are thy thoughts, O child of mortal birth!
And impotent thy tongue. Is thy short span
Capacious of this universal frame?

Thy wisdom all-sufficient? Thou, alas!
Dost thou aspire to judge between the Lord
Of Nature and his works? to lift thy voice
Against the sovereign order he decreed,
All good and lovely? to blaspheme the bands
Of tenderness innate, and social love,
Holiest of things! by which the general orb
Of being, as by adamantine links,
Was drawn to perfect union, and sustain'd
From everlasting? Hast thou felt the pangs
Of softening sorrow, of indignant zeal,
So grievous to the soul, as thence to wish
The ties of Nature broken from thy frame;
That so thy selfish, unrelenting heart
Might cease to mourn its lot, no longer then
The wretched heir of evils not its own?
O fair benevolence of generous minds!
O man by Nature form'd for all mankind!'

"He spoke; abash'd and silent I remain'd,
As conscious of my tongue's offence, and awed
Before his presence, though my secret soul
Disdain'd the imputation. On the ground
I fix'd my eyes; till from his airy couch
He stoop'd sublime, and touching with his hand
My dazzling forehead, 'Raise thy sight,' he cried,
'And let thy sense convince thy erring tongue.'

"I look'd, and lo! the former scene was changed;
For verdant alleys and surrounding trees,

A solitary prospect, wide and wild,
Rush'd on my senses. 'T was an horrid pile
Of hills, with many a shaggy forest mix'd,
With many a sable cliff and glittering stream.
Aloft, recumbent o'er the hanging ridge,
The brown woods waved; while ever-trickling springs
Wash'd from the naked roots of oak and pine
The crumbling soil; and still at every fall
Down the steep windings of the channel'd rock,
Remurmuring rush'd the congregated floods
With hoarser inundation; till at last
They reach'd a grassy plain, which from the skirts
Of that high desert spread her verdant lap,
And drank the gushing moisture, where, confined
In one smooth current, o'er the lilied vale
Clearer than glass it flow'd. Autumnal spoils,
Luxuriant spreading to the rays of morn,
Blush'd o'er the cliffs, whose half encircling mound
As in a sylvan theatre inclosed
That flowery level. On the river's brink
I spied a fair pavilion, which diffused
Its floating umbrage 'mid the silver shade
Of osiers. Now the western Sun reveal'd
Between two parting cliffs his golden orb,
And pour'd across the shadow of the hills,
On rocks and floods, a yellow stream of light
That cheer'd the solemn scene. My listening powers
Were awed, and every thought in silence hung,

And wondering expectation. Then the voice
Of that celestial power, the mystic show
Declaring thus my deep attention call'd.

"'Inhabitants of Earth, to whom is given
The gracious ways of Providence to learn,
Receive my sayings with a steadfast ear—
Know then, the sovereign Spirit of the world,
Though, self-collected from eternal time,
Within his own deep essence he beheld
The bounds of true felicity complete;
Yet by immense benignity inclined
To spread around him that primeval joy
Which fill'd himself, he raised his plastic arm,
And sounded through the hollow depth of space
The strong, creative mandate. Straight arose
These heavenly orbs, the glad abodes of life
Effusive kindled by his breath divine
Through endless forms of being. Each inhaled
From him its portion of the vital flame,
In measure such, that, from the wide complex
Of coexistent orders, one might rise,
One Order, all-involving and entire,
He too beholding in the sacred light
Of his essential reason, all the shapes
Of swift contingence, all successive ties
Of action propagated through the sum
Of possible existence, he at once,
Down the long series of eventful time,

So fix'd the dates of being, so disposed,
To every living soul of every kind
The field of motion and the hour of rest,
That all conspired to his supreme design,
To universal good: with full accord
Answering the mighty model he had chosen,
The best and fairest of unnumber'd worlds,
That lay from everlasting in the store
Of his divine conceptions. Nor content,
By one exertion of creative power
His goodness to reveal; through every age,
Through every moment up the tract of time,
His parent-hand, with ever-new increase
Of happiness and virtue, has adorn'd
The vast harmonious frame: his parent-hand,
From the mute shell-fish gasping on the shore,
To men, to angels, to celestial minds,
For ever leads the generations on
To higher scenes of being; while, supplied
From day to day with his enlivening breath,
Inferior orders in succession rise
To fill the void below. As flame ascends,
As bodies to their proper centre move,
As the poised ocean to the attracting Moon
Obedient swells, and every headlong stream
Devolves its winding waters to the main;
So all things which have life aspire to God,
The sun of being, boundless, unimpair'd,
Centre of souls! Nor does the faithful voice

Of Nature cease to prompt their eager steps
Aright; nor is the care of Heaven withheld
From granting to the task proportion'd aid;
That in their stations all may persevere
To climb the ascent of being, and approach
For ever nearer to the life divine.

"'That rocky pile thou see'st, that verdant lawn,
Fresh-water'd from the mountains. Let the scene
Paint in thy fancy the primeval seat
Of man, and where the will supreme ordain'd
His mansion, that pavilion fair diffused
Along the shady brink; in this recess
To wear the appointed season of his youth,
Till riper hours should open to his toil
The high communion of superior minds
Of consecrated heroes and of gods.
Nor did the Sire Omnipotent forget
His tender bloom to cherish; nor withheld
Celestial footsteps from his green abode.
Oft from the radiant honours of his throne,
He sent whom most he loved, the sovereign fair,
The effluence of his glory, whom he placed
Before his eyes for ever to behold;
The goddess from whose inspiration flows
The toil of patriots, the delight of friends,
Without whose work divine, in Heaven or Earth,
Naught lovely, naught propitious, comes to pass,
Nor hope, nor praise, nor honour. Her the Sire

Gave it in charge to rear the blooming mind,
The folded powers to open, to direct
The growth luxuriant of his young desires,
And from the laws of this majestic world
To teach him what was good. As thus the nymph
Her daily care attended, by her side
With constant steps her gay companions stay'd,
The fair Euphrosyné, the gentle queen
Of smiles, and graceful gladness, and delights
That cheer alike the hearts of mortal men
And powers immortal. See the shining pair!
Behold, where from his dwelling now disclosed,
They quit their youthful charge and seek the skies.'

"I look'd, and on the flowery turf there stood,
Between two radiant forms, a smiling youth,
Whose tender cheeks display'd the vernal flower
Of beauty; sweetest innocence illumed
His bashful eyes, and on his polish'd brow
Sate young Simplicity. With fond regard
He view'd the associates, as their steps they moved
The younger chief his ardent eyes detain'd,
With mild regret invoking her return.
Bright as the star of evening she appear'd
Amid the dusky scene. Eternal youth
O'er all her form its glowing honours breathed;
And smiles eternal from her candid eyes
Flow'd, like the dewy lustre of the morn
Effusive trembling on the placid waves.

The spring of Heaven had shed its blushing spoils
To bind her sable tresses: full diffused
Her yellow mantle floated in the breeze;
And in her hand she waved a living branch
Rich with immortal fruits, of power to calm
The wrathful heart, and from the brightening eyes
To chase the cloud of sadness. More sublime
The heavenly partner moved. The prime of age
Composed her steps. The presence of a god,
High on the circle of her brow enthroned,
From each majestic motion darted awe,
Devoted awe! till, cherish'd by her looks
Benevolent and meet, confiding love
To filial rapture soften'd all the soul.
Free in her graceful hand she poised the sword
Of chaste dominion. An heroic crown
Display'd the old simplicity of pomp
Around her honour'd head. A matron's robe,
White as the sunshine streams through vernal clouds,
Her stately form invested. Hand in hand
The immortal pair forsook the enamel'd green,
Ascending slowly. Rays of limpid light
Gleam'd round their path; celestial sounds were
heard,
And through the fragrant air ethereal dews
Distill'd around them; till at once the clouds
Disparting wide in midway sky withdrew
Their airy veil, and left a bright expanse
Of empyréan flame, where, spent and drown'd,

Afflicted vision plunged in vain to scan
What object it involved. My feeble eyes
Endured not. Bending down to earth, I stood,
With dumb attention. Soon a female voice,
As watery murmurs sweet, or warbling shades,
With sacred invocation thus began.

"'Father of gods and mortals! whose right arm
With reins eternal guides the moving heavens,
Bend thy propitious ear. Behold well-pleased
I seek to finish thy divine decree.
With frequent steps I visit yonder seat
Of man, thy offspring; from the tender seeds
Of justice and of wisdom, to evolve
The latent honours of his generous frame;
Till thy conducting hand shall raise his lot
From earth's dim scene to these ethereal walks,
The temple of thy glory. But not me,
Not my directing voice, he oft requires,
Or hears delighted: this enchanting maid,
The associate thou hast given me, her alone
He loves, O Father! absent, her he craves;
And but for her glad presence ever join'd,
Rejoices not in mine: that all my hopes
This thy benignant purpose to fulfil,
I deem uncertain: and my daily cares
Unfruitful all and vain, unless by thee
Still further aided in the work divine.'

"She ceased; a voice more awful thus replied.
'O thou! in whom for ever I delight,
Fairer than all the inhabitants of Heaven,
Best image of thy author! far from thee
Be disappointment, or distaste, or blame;
Who, soon or late, shall every work fulfil,
And no resistance find. If man refuse
To hearken to thy dictates; or allured
By meaner joys, to any other power
Transfer the honours due to thee alone;
That joy which he pursues he ne'er shall taste,
That power in whom delighteth ne'er behold.
Go then, once more, and happy be thy toil:
Go then! but let not this thy smiling friend
Partake thy footsteps. In her stead, behold!
With thee the son of Nemesis I send;
The fiend abhorr'd! whose vengeance takes account
Of sacred Order's violated laws.
See where he calls thee, burning to be gone,
Fierce to exhaust the tempest of his wrath
On yon devoted head. But thou, my child,
Control his cruel frenzy, and protect
Thy tender charge; that when Despair shall grasp
His agonizing bosom, he may learn,
Then he may learn to love the gracious hand
Alone sufficient in the hour of ill
To save his feeble spirit; then confess
Thy genuine honours, O excelling fair!
When all the plagues that wait the deadly wi'

Of this avenging demon, all the storms
Of night infernal, serve but to display
The energy of thy superior charms
With mildest awe triumphant o'er his rage,
And shining clearer in the horrid gloom.'

"Here ceased that awful voice, and soon I felt
The cloudy curtain of refreshing eve
Was closed once more, from that immortal fire
Sheltering my eyelids. Looking up, I view'd
A vast gigantic spectre striding on
Through murmuring thunders and a waste of clouds,
With dreadful action. Black as night, his brow
Relentless frowns involved. His savage limbs
With sharp impatience violent he writhed,
As through convulsive anguish; and his hand,
Arm'd with a scorpion-lash, full oft he raised
In madness to his bosom; while his eyes
Rain'd bitter tears, and bellowing loud, he shook
The void with horror. Silent by his side
The virgin came. No discomposure stirr'd
Her features. From the glooms which hung around
No stain of darkness mingled with the beam
Of her divine effulgence. Now they stoop
Upon the river-bank; and now, to hail
His wonted guests, with eager steps advanced
The unsuspecting inmate of the shade.

"As when a famish'd wolf, that all night long
Had ranged the Alpine snows, by chance at morn

Sees from a cliff incumbent o'er the smoke
Of some lone village, a neglected kid
That strays along the wild for herb or spring;
Down from the winding ridge he sweeps amain,
And thinks he tears him: so with tenfold rage,
The monster sprung remorseless on his prey.
Amazed the stripling stood: with panting breast
Feebly he pour'd the lamentable wail
Of helpless consternation, struck at once,
And rooted to the ground. The queen beheld
His terror, and with looks of tenderest care
Advanced to save him. Soon the tyrant felt
Her awful power. His keen, tempestuous arm
Hung nerveless, nor descended where his rage
Had aim'd the deadly blow: then dumb retired
With sullen rancour. Lo! the sovran maid
Folds with a mother's arms the fainting boy,
Till life rekindles in his rosy cheek;
Then grasps his hands, and cheers him with her tongue.

"'O wake thee, rouse thy spirit! Shall the spite
Of yon tormenter thus appal thy heart,
While I, thy friend and guardian, am at hand
To rescue and to heal? O let thy soul
Remember, what the will of Heaven ordains
Is ever good for all; and if for all,
Then good for thee. Nor only by the warmth
And soothing sunshine of delightful things,

Do minds grow up and flourish. Oft misled
By that bland light, the young unpractised views
Of reason wander through a fatal road,
Far from their native aim; as if to lie
Inglorious in the fragant shade, and wait
The soft access of ever-circling joys,
Were all the end of being. Ask thyself,
This pleasing error did it never lull
Thy wishes? Has thy constant heart refused
The silken fetters of delicious ease?
Or when divine Euphrosyné appear'd
Within this dwelling, did not thy desires
Hang far below the measure of thy fate,
Which I reveal'd before thee? and thy eyes,
Impatient of my counsels, turn away
To drink the soft effusion of her smiles?
Know then, for this the everlasting Sire
Deprives thee of her presence, and instead,
O wise and still benevolent! ordains
This horrid visage hither to pursue
My steps; that so thy nature may discern
Its real good, and what alone can save
Thy feeble spirit in this hour of ill
From folly and despair. O yet beloved!
Let not this headlong terror quite o'erwhelm
Thy scatter'd powers; nor fatal deem the rage
Of this tormenter, nor his proud assault,
While I am here to vindicate thy toil
Above the generous question of thy arm.

Brave by thy fears, and in thy weakness strong,
This hour he triumphs; but confront his might,
And dare him to the combat, then with ease
Disarm'd and quell'd, his fierceness he resigns
To bondage and to scorn; while thus inured
By watchful danger, by unceasing toil,
The immortal mind, superior to his fate,
Amid the outrage of external things,
Firm as the solid base of this great world,
Rests on his own foundations. Blow, ye winds!
Ye waves! ye thunders! roll your tempest on;
Shake, ye old pillars of the marble sky!
Till all its orbs and all its worlds of fire
Be loosen'd from their seats; yet still serene,
The unconquer'd mind looks down upon the wreck;
And ever stronger as the storms advance,
Firm through the closing ruin holds his way,
Where Nature calls him to the destined goal.'

"So spake the goddess; while through all her frame
Celestial raptures flow'd, in every word,
In every motion kindling warmth divine
To seize who listen'd. Vehement and swift,
As lightning fires the aromatic shade
In Ethiopian fields, the stripling felt
Her inspiration catch his fervid soul,
And, starting from his languor, thus exclaim'd:

"'Then let the trial come! and witness thou,
If terror be upon me; if I shrink
To meet the storm, or falter in my strength
When hardest it besets me. Do not think
That I am fearful and infirm of soul,
As late thy eyes beheld; for thou hast changed
My nature; thy commanding voice has waked
My languid powers to bear me boldly on,
Where'er the will divine my path ordains
Through toil or peril: only do not thou
Forsake me; O be thou for ever near,
That I may listen to thy sacred voice,
And guide by thy decrees my constant feet.
But say, for ever are my eyes bereft?
Say, shall the fair Euphrosyné not once
Appear again to charm me? Thou, in Heaven!
O thou eternal arbiter of things!
Be thy great bidding done: for who am I,
To question thy appointment? Let the frowns
Of this avenger every morn o'ercast
The cheerful dawn, and every evening damp
With double night my dwelling; I will learn
To hail them both, and unrepining bear
His hateful presence; but permit my tongue
One glad request, and if my deeds may find
Thy awful eye propitious, O restore
The rosy-featured maid, again to cheer
This lonely seat, and bless me with her smiles.'

14

"He spoke; when instant through the sable glooms
With which that furious presence had involved
The ambient air, a flood of radiance came
Swift as the lightning flash; the melting clouds
Flew diverse, and amid the blue serene
Euphrosyné appear'd. With sprightly step
The nymph alighted on the irriguous lawn,
And to her wondering audience thus began.

"'Lo! I am here to answer to your vows,
And be the meeting fortunate! I come
With joyful tidings; we shall part no more.—
Hark! how the gentle Echo from her cell
Talks through the cliffs, and murmuring o'er the stream
Repeats the accents—we shall part no more.
O my delightful friends! well-pleased on high
The Father has beheld you, while the might
Of that stern foe with bitter trial proved
Your equal doings; then for ever spake
The high decree: That thou, celestial maid!
Howe'er that grisly phantom on thy steps
May sometimes dare intrude, yet never more
Shalt thou, descending to the abode of man,
Alone endure the rancour of his arm,
Or leave thy loved Euphrosyné behind.'

"She ended; and the whole romantic scene
Immediate vanish'd; rocks, and woods, and rills,

The mantling tent, and each mysterious form,
Flew like the pictures of a morning dream,
When sunshine fills the bed. Awhile I stood
Perplex'd and giddy; till the radiant power
Who bade the visionary landscape rise,
As up to him I turn'd, with gentlest looks
Preventing my inquiry, thus began.

"'There let thy soul acknowledge its complaint
How blind! how impious! There behold the ways
Of Heaven's eternal destiny to man,
For ever just, benevolent, and wise:
That Virtue's awful steps, howe'er pursued
By vexing Fortune and intrusive Pain,
Should never be divided from her chaste,
Her fair attendant, Pleasure. Need I urge
Thy tardy thought through all the various round
Of this existence, that thy softening soul
At length may learn what energy the hand
Of Virtue mingles in the bitter tide
Of passion, swelling with distress and pain,
To mitigate the sharp with gracious drops
Of cordial pleasure? Ask the faithful youth
Why the cold urn of her whom long he loved
So often fills his arms; so often draws
His lonely footsteps at the silent hour,
To pay the mournful tribute of his tears?
Oh! he will tell thee, that the wealth of worlds
Should ne'er seduce his bosom to forego

That sacred hour, when, stealing from the noise
Of care and envy, sweet remembrance soothes
With Virtue's kindest looks his aching breast,
And turns his tears to rapture.—Ask the crowd
Which flies impatient from the village-walk
To climb the neighbouring cliffs, when far below
The cruel winds have hurl'd upon the coast
Some helpless bark; while sacred Pity melts
The general eye, or Terror's icy hand
Smites their distorted limbs and horrent hair:
While every mother closer to her breast
Catches her child, and, pointing where the waves
Foam through the shatter'd vessel, shrieks aloud,
As one poor wretch that spreads his piteous arms
For succour, swallow'd by the roaring surge,
As now another, dash'd against the rock,
Drops lifeless down: O! deemest thou indeed
No kind endearment here by Nature given
To mutual terror and Compassion's tears?
No sweetly-melting softness which attracts,
O'er all that edge of pain, the social powers
To this their proper action and their end?
—Ask thy own heart; when at the midnight hour,
Slow through that studious gloom thy pausing eye,
Led by the glimmering taper, moves around
The sacred volumes of the dead, the songs
Of Grecian bards, and records writ by Fame
For Grecian heroes, where the present power
Of heaven and earth surveys th' immortal page,

Even as a father blessing, while he reads
The praises of his son. If then thy soul,
Spurning the yoke of these inglorious days,
Mix in their deeds and kindle with their flame;
Say, when the prospect blackens on thy view,
When rooted from the base, heroic states
Mourn in the dust, and tremble at the frown
Of curst Ambition; when the pious band
Of youths who fought for freedom and their sires,
Lie side by side in gore; when ruffian Pride
Usurps the throne of Justice, turns the pomp
Of public power, the majesty of rule,
The sword, the laurel, and the purple robe,
To slavish, empty pageants, to adorn
A tyrant's walk, and glitter in the eyes
Of such as bow the knee; when honour'd urns
Of patriots and of chiefs, the awful bust
And storied arch, to glut the coward rage
Of regal Envy, strew the public way
With hallow'd ruins; when the Muse's haunt,
The marble porch where Wisdom wont to talk
With SOCRATES or TULLY, hears no more,
Save the hoarse jargon of contentious monks,
Or female superstition's midnight prayer;
When ruthless Rapine from the hand of Time
Tears the destroying scythe, with surer blow
To sweep the works of glory from their base;
Till Desolation o'er the grass-grown street
Expands his raven-wings, and up the wall,

Where senates once the price of monarchs doom'd
Hisses the gliding snake through hoary weeds
That clasp the mouldering column; thus defaced,
Thus widely mournful when the prospect thrills
Thy beating bosom, when the patriot's tear
Starts from thine eye, and thy extended arm
In fancy hurls the thunderbolt of Jove,
To fire the impious wreath on Philip's brow,
Or dash Octavius from the trophied car;
Say, does thy secret soul repine to taste
The big distress? Or wouldst thou then exchange
Those heart-ennobling sorrows for the lot
Of him who sits amid the gaudy herd
Of mute barbarians bending to his nod,
And bears aloft his gold-invested front,
And says within himself—I am a king,
And wherefore should the clamorous voice of woe
Intrude upon mine ear?—The baleful dregs
Of these late ages, this inglorious draught
Of servitude and folly, have not yet,
Blest be the eternal Ruler of the world!
Defiled to such a depth of sordid shame
The native honours of the human soul,
Nor so effaced the image of its sire.'"

AKENSIDE'S

PLEASURES OF IMAGINATION.

BOOK III.

ARGUMENT.

Pleasure in observing the tempers and manners of men, even where vicious or absurd. The origin of vice, from false representations of the fancy, producing false opinions concerning good and evil. Inquiry into ridicule. The general sources of ridicule in the minds and characters of men, enumerated. Final cause of the sense of ridicule. The resemblance of certain aspects of inanimate things to the sensations and properties of the mind. The operations of the mind in the production of the works of imagination, described. The secondary pleasure from imitation. The benevolent order of the world illustrated in the arbitrary connexion of these pleasures with the objects which excite them. The nature and conduct of taste. Concluding with an account of the natural and moral advantages resulting from a sensible and well-formed imagination.

THE

PLEASURES OF IMAGINATION.

BOOK III.

What wonder, therefore, since the endearing ties
Of passion link the universal kind
Of man so close, what wonder if to search
This common nature through the various change
Of sex, and age, and fortune, and the frame
Of each peculiar, draw the busy mind
With unresisted charms? The spacious west,
And all the teeming regions of the south,
Hold not a quarry, to the curious flight
Of knowledge, half so tempting or so fair,
As man to man. Nor only where the smiles
Of Love invite; nor only where the applause
Of cordial Honour turns the attentive eye
On Virtue's graceful deeds. For since the course
Of things external acts in different ways
On human apprehensions, as the hand
Of Nature temper'd to a different frame
Peculiar minds; so haply where the powers
Of Fancy neither lessen nor enlarge
The images of things, but paint, in all

Their genuine hues, the features which they wore
In Nature; there Opinion will be true,
And Action right. For Action treads the path
In which Opinion says he follows good,
Or flies from evil; and Opinion gives
Report of good or evil, as the scene
Was drawn by Fancy, lovely or deform'd:
Thus her report can never there be true,
Where Fancy cheats the intellectual eye
With glaring colours and distorted lines.
Is there a man, who at the sound of Death
Sees ghastly shapes of terror conjured up,
And black before him; naught but death-bed groans
And fearful prayers, and plunging from the brink
Of light and being, down the gloomy air
An unknown depth? Alas! in such a mind,
If no bright forms of excellence attend
The image of his country; nor the pomp
Of sacred senates, nor the guardian voice
Of Justice on her throne, nor aught that wakes
The conscious bosom with a patriot's flame;
Will not Opinion tell him, that to die,
Or stand the hazard, is a greater ill
Than to betray his country? And in act
Will he not choose to be a wretch, and live?
Here vice begins then. From the enchanting cup
Which Fancy holds to all, the unwary thirst
Of youth oft swallows a Circæan draught,
That sheds a baleful tincture o'er the eye

Of Reason, till no longer he discerns,
And only guides to err. Then revel forth
A furious band that spurns him from the throne
And all is uproar. Thus Ambition grasps
The empire of the soul: thus pale Revenge
Unsheaths her murderous dagger; and the hands
Of Lust and Rapine, with unholy arts,
Watch to o'erturn the barrier of the laws
That keeps them from their prey: thus all the plagues
The wicked bear, or o'er the trembling scene
The tragic Muse discloses, under shapes
Of honour, safety, pleasure, ease, or pomp,
Stole first into the mind. Yet not by all
Those lying forms which Fancy in the brain
Engenders, are the kindling passions driven
To guilty deeds; nor Reason bound in chains,
That Vice alone may lord it; oft adorn'd
With solemn pageants, folly mounts the throne,
And plays her idiot-antics, like a queen.
A thousand garbs she wears; a thousand ways
She wheels her giddy empire.—Lo! thus far
With bold adventure, to the Mantuan lyre
I sing of Nature's charms, and touch well-pleased
A stricter note; now haply must my song
Unbend her serious measure, and reveal
In lighter strains, how Folly's awkward arts
Excite impetuous Laughter's gay rebuke;
The sportive province of the comic Muse.

See! in what crowds the uncouth forms advance:
Each would outstrip the other, each prevent
Our careful search, and offer to your gaze,
Unmask'd, his motley features. Wait awhile,
My curious friends! and let us first arrange,
In proper order, your promiscuous throng.

Behold the foremost band; of slender thought,
And easy faith; whom flattering Fancy soothes
With lying spectres, in themselves to view
Illustrious forms of excellence and good,
That scorn the mansion. With exulting hearts
They spread their spurious treasures to the Sun,
And bid the world admire! but chief the glance
Of wishful Envy draws their joy-bright eyes,
And lifts with self-applause each lordly brow.
In numbers boundless as the blooms of spring,
Behold their glaring idols, empty shades
By Fancy gilded o'er, and then set up
For adoration. Some in Learning's garb,
With formal band, and sable-cinctured gown,
And rags of mouldy volumes. Some elate
With martial splendour, steely pikes and swords
Of costly frame, and gay Phœnician robes
Inwrought with flowery gold, assume the port
Of stately Valour: listening by his side
There stands a female form; to her, with looks
Of earnest import, pregnant with amaze,
He talks of deadly deeds, of breaches, storms,

And sulphurous mines, and ambush: then at once
Breaks off, and smiles to see her look so pale,
And asks some wondering question of her fears.
Others of graver mien; behold, adorn'd
With holy ensigns, how sublime they move,
And, bending oft their sanctimonious eyes,
Take homage of the simple-minded throng;
Ambassadors of Heaven! Nor much unlike
Is he whose visage, in the lazy mist
That mantles every feature, hides a brood
Of politic conceits; of whispers, nods,
And hints deep-omen'd with unwieldy schemes,
And dark portents of state. Ten thousand more
Prodigious habits and tumultuous tongues,
Pour dauntless in, and swell the boastful band.

Then comes the second order, all who seek
The debt of praise, where watchful Unbelief
Darts through the thin pretence her squinting eye
On some retired appearance, which belies
The boasted virtue, or annuls the applause
That Justice else would pay. Here side by side
I see two leaders of the solemn train
Approaching: one a female old and gray,
With eyes demure, and wrinkle-furrow'd brow,
Pale as the cheeks of Death; yet still she stuns
The sickening audience with a nauseous tale;
How many youths her myrtle chains have worn,
How many virgins at her triumphs pined!

Yet how resolved she guards her cautious heart;
Such is her terror at the risks of love,
And man's seducing tongue! The other seems
A bearded sage, ungentle in his mien,
And sordid all his habit; peevish Want
Grins at his heels, while down the gazing throng
He stalks, resounding in magnific phrase
The vanity of riches, the contempt
Of pomp and power. Be prudent in your zeal,
Ye grave associates! let the silent grace
Of her who blushes at the fond regard
Her charms inspire, more eloquent unfold
The praise of spotless honour: let the man
Whose eye regards not his illustrious pomp
And ample store, but as indulgent streams
To cheer the barren soil and spread the fruits
Of joy, let him by juster measures fix
The price of riches and the end of power.

Another tribe succeeds; deluded long
By Fancy's dazzling optics, these behold
The images of some peculiar things
With brighter hues resplendent, and portray'd
With features nobler far than e'er adorn'd
Their genuine objects. Hence the fever'd heart
Pants with delirious hope for tinsel charms;
Hence oft, obtrusive on the eye of Scorn,
Untimely Zeal her witless pride betrays!
And serious manhood from the towering aim

Of Wisdom, stoops to emulate the boast
Of childish toil. Behold yon mystic form,
Bedeck'd with feathers, insects, weeds, and shells!
Not with intenser view the Samian sage
Bent his fix'd eye on Heaven's intenser fires,
When first the order of that radiant scene
Swell'd his exulting thought, than this surveys
A muckworm's entrails or a spider's fang.
Next him a youth, with flowers and myrtles crown'd,
Attends that virgin form, and blushing kneels,
With fondest gesture and a suppliant's tongue,
To win her coy regard: adieu, for him,
The dull engagements of the bustling world!
Adieu the sick impertinence of praise!
And hope, and action! for with her alone,
By streams and shades, to steal these sighing hours
Is all he asks, and all that Fate can give!
Thee too, facetious Momion, wandering here,
Thee, dreaded censor, oft have I beheld
Bewilder'd unawares: alas! too long
Flush'd with thy comic triumphs and the spoils
Of sly Derision! till on every side
Hurling thy random bolts, offended Truth
Assign'd thee here thy station with the slaves
Of Folly. Thy once formidable name
Shall grace her humble records, and be heard
In scoffs and mockery, bandied from the lips
Of all the vengeful brotherhood around,
So oft the patient victims of thy scorn.

But now, ye gay! to whom indulgent Fate,
Of all the Muse's empire, hath assign'd
The fields of folly, hither each advance
Your sickles; here the teeming soil affords
Its richest growth. A favourite brood appears
In whom the demon, with a mother's joy,
Views all her charms reflected, all her cares
At full repaid. Ye most illustrious band!
Who, scorning Reason's tame, pedantic rules,
And Order's vulgar bondage, never meant
For souls sublime as yours, with generous zeal
Pay Vice the reverence Virtue long usurp'd,
And yield Deformity the fond applause
Which Beauty wont to claim; forgive my song,
That for the blushing diffidence of youth,
It shuns the unequal province of your praise.

Thus far triumphant in the pleasing guile
Of bland Imagination, Folly's train
Have dared our search; but now a dastard kind
Advance reluctant, and with faltering feet
Shrink from the gazer's eye; enfeebled hearts
Whom Fancy chills with visionary fears,
Or bends to servile tameness with conceits
Of shame, of evil, or of base defect,
Fantastic and delusive. Here the slave
Who droops abash'd when sullen Pomp surveys
His humbler habit; here the trembling wretch
Unnerved and struck with Terror's icy bolts,

Spent in weak wailings, drown'd in shameful tears,
At every dream of danger; here subdued
By frontless Laughter, and the hardy scorn
Of old, unfeeling Vice, the abject soul,
Who blushing half resigns the candid praise
Of Temperance and Honour; half disowns
A freeman's hatred of tyrannic pride;
And hears with sickly smiles the venal mouth
With foulest license mock the patriot's name.

Last of the motley bands on whom the power
Of gay Derision bends her hostile aim,
Is that where shameful Ignorance presides.
Beneath her sordid banners, lo! they march,
Like blind and lame. Whate'er their doubtful hand
Attempt, Confusion straight appears behind,
And troubles all the work. Through many a maze,
Perplex'd they struggle, changing every path,
O'erturning every purpose; then at last
Sit down dismay'd, and leave the entangled scene
For Scorn to sport with. Such then is the abode
Of Folly in the mind; and such the shapes
In which she governs her obsequious train.

Through every scene of ridicule in things
To lead the tenour of my devious lay;
Through every swift occasion, which the hand
Of Laughter points at, when the mirthful sting
Distends her sallying nerves and chokes her tongue;

What were it but to count each crystal drop
Which Morning's dewy fingers on the blooms
Of May distil? Suffice it to have said,
Where'er the power of Ridicule displays
Her quaint-eyed visage, some incongruous form,
Some stubborn dissonance of things combined,
Strikes on the quick observer: whether Pomp,
Or Praise, or Beauty, mix their partial claim
Where sordid fashions, where ignoble deeds,
Where foul deformity are wont to dwell;
Or whether these with violation loth'd,
Invade resplendent Pomp's imperious mien,
The charms of Beauty, or the boast of Praise.

Ask we for what fair end, the Almighty Sire
In mortal bosoms wakes this gay contempt,
These grateful stings of laughter, from disgust
Educing pleasure? Wherefore, but to aid
The tardy steps of Reason, and at once
By this prompt impulse urge us to depress
The giddy aims of Folly? Though the light
Of Truth, slow dawning on the inquiring mind,
At length unfolds, through many a subtle tie,
How these uncouth disorders end at last
In public evil; yet benignant Heaven,
Conscious how dim the dawn of Truth appears
To thousands; conscious what a scanty pause
From labours and from care, the wider lot
Of humble life affords for studious thought

To scan the maze of Nature; therefore stamp'd
The glaring scenes with characters of scorn,
As broad, as obvious, to the passing clown,
As to the letter'd sage's curious eye.

Such are the various aspects of the mind—
Some heavenly genius, whose unclouded thoughts
Attain that secret harmony which blends
The ethereal spirit with its mould of clay;
O! teach me to reveal the graceful charm
That searchless Nature o'er the sense of man
Diffuses, to behold, in lifeless things,
The inexpressive semblance of himself,
Of thought and passion. Mark the sable woods
That shade sublime yon mountain's nodding brow;
With what religious awe the solemn scene
Commands your steps! as if the reverend form
Of Minos or of Numa should forsake
The Elysian seats, and down the embowering glade
Move to your pausing eye! Behold the expanse
Of yon gay landscape, where the silver clouds
Flit o'er the heavens before the sprightly breeze:
Now their gray cincture skirts the doubtful Sun;
Now streams of splendour, through their opening veil
Effulgent, sweep from off the gilded lawn
The aërial shadows; on the curling brook,
And on the shady margin's quivering leaves
With quickest lustre glancing; while you view
The prospect, say, within your cheerful breast

Plays not the lively sense of winning mirth
With clouds and sunshine chequer'd, while the round
Of social converse, to the inspiring tongue
Of some gay nymph amid her subject train,
Moves all obsequious? Whence is this effect,
This kindred power of such discordant things?
Or flows their semblance from that mystic tone
To which the new-born mind's harmonious powers
At first were strung? Or rather from the links
Which artful custom twines around her frame?

For when the different images of things,
By chance combined, have struck the attentive soul
With deeper impulse, or connected long,
Have drawn her frequent eye; howe'er distinct
The external scenes, yet oft the ideas gain
From that conjunction an eternal tie,
And sympathy unbroken. Let the mind
Recall one partner of the various league,
Immediate, lo! the firm confederates rise,
And each his former station straight resumes:
One movement governs the consenting throng,
And all at once with rosy pleasures shine,
Or all are sadden'd with the glooms of care.
'T was thus, if ancient Fame the truth unfold,
Two faithful needles, from the informing touch
Of the same parent-stone, together drew
Its mystic virtue, and at first conspired
With fatal impulse quivering to the Pole;

Then, though disjoin'd by kingdoms, though the main
Roll'd its broad surge betwixt, and different stars
Beheld their wakeful motions, yet preserved
The former friendship, and remember'd still
The alliance of their birth: whate'er the line
Which once possess'd, nor pause, nor quiet knew
The sure associate, ere with trembling speed
He found its path, and fix'd unerring there.
Such is the secret union, when we feel
A song, a flower, a name, at once restore
Those long connected scenes where first they moved
The attention: backward through her mazy walks
Guiding the wanton Fancy to her scope,
To temples, courts, or fields; with all the band
Of painted forms, of passions and designs
Attendant: whence, if pleasing in itself,
The prospect from that sweet accession gains
Redoubled influence o'er the listening mind.

By these mysterious ties the busy power
Of Memory her ideal train preserves
Entire; or when they would elude her watch,
Reclaims their fleeting footsteps from the waste
Of dark oblivion; thus collecting all
The various forms of being, to present,
Before the curious aim of mimic Art,
Their largest choice; like Spring's unfolded blooms
Exhaling sweetness, that the skilful bee
May taste at will from their selected spoils

To work her dulcet food. For not the expanse
Of living lakes in Summer's noontide calm,
Reflects the bordering shade, and sun-bright heavens,
With fairer semblance; not the sculptured gold
More faithful keeps the graver's lively trace,
Than he, whose birth the sister powers of Art
Propitious view'd, and from his genial star
Shed influence to the seeds of fancy kind;
Than his attemper'd bosom must preserve
The seal of Nature. There alone unchanged,
Her form remains. The balmy walks of May
There breathe perennial sweets: the trembling chord
Resounds for ever in the abstracted ear,
Melodious: and the virgin's radiant eye,
Superior to disease, to grief, and time,
Shines with unbating lustre. Thus at length
Endow'd with all that Nature can bestow,
The child of Fancy oft in silence bends
O'er these mixt treasures of his pregnant breast,
With conscious pride. From them he oft resolves
To frame he knows not what excelling things;
And win he knows not what sublime reward
Of praise and wonder. By degrees, the mind
Feels her young nerves dilate: the plastic powers
Labour for action: blind emotions heave
His bosom, and with loveliest frenzy caught,
From earth to heaven he rolls his daring eye,
From heaven to earth. Anon ten thousand shapes,
Like spectres trooping to the wizard's call,

Flit swift before him. From the womb of Earth,
From Ocean's bed, they come; the eternal Heavens
Disclose their splendours, and the dark Abyss
Pours out her births unknown. With fixed gaze
He marks the rising phantoms. Now compares
Their different forms; now blends them, now divides
Enlarges, and extenuates by turns;
Opposes, ranges in fantastic bands,
And infinitely varies. Hither now,
Now thither fluctuates his inconstant aim,
With endless choice perplex'd. At length his plan
Begins to open. Lucid order dawns;
And as from Chaos old the jarring seeds
Of Nature at the voice divine repair'd
Each to its place, till rosy Earth unveil'd
Her fragrant bosom, and the joyful Sun
Sprung up the blue serene; by swift degrees
Thus disentangled, his entire design
Emerges. Colours mingle, features join;
And lines converge: the fainter parts retire;
The fairer eminent in light advance;
And every image on its neighbour smiles.
Awhile he stands, and with a father's joy
Contemplates. Then with Prometheán art,
Into its proper vehicle he breathes
The fair conception; which, embodied thus.
And permanent, becomes to eyes or ears
An object ascertain'd; while thus inform'd,
The various organs of his mimic skill,

The consonance of sounds, the featured rock,
The shadowy picture and impassion'd verse,
Beyond their proper powers attract the soul
By that expressive semblance, while in sight
Of Nature's great original we scan
The lively child of Art; while line by line,
And feature after feature, we refer
To that sublime exemplar whence it stole
Those animating charms. Thus beauty's palm
Betwixt them wavering hangs: applauding love
Doubts where to choose; and mortal man aspires
To tempt creative praise. As when a cloud
Of gathering hail, with limpid crusts of ice
Inclosed and obvious to the beaming Sun,
Collects his large effulgence; straight the heavens
With equal flames present on either hand
The radiant visage: Persia stands at gaze,
Appall'd; and on the brink of Ganges doubts
The snowy-vested seer, in MITHRA'S name,
To which the fragrance of the south shall burn,
To which his warbled orisons ascend.

Such various bliss the well-tuned heart enjoys,
Favour'd of Heaven! while, plunged in sordid cares,
The unfeeling vulgar mocks the boon divine:
And harsh Austerity, from whose rebuke
Young Love and smiling Wonder shrink away
Abash'd, and chill of heart, with sager frowns
Condemns the fair enchantment. On my strain,

Perhaps even now, some cold fastidious judge
Casts a disdainful eye; and calls my toil,
And calls the love and beauty which I sing,
The dream of folly. Thou, grave censor! say,
Is Beauty then a dream, because the glooms
Of dullness hang too heavy on thy sense
To let her shine upon thee? So the man
Whose eye ne'er open'd on the light of Heaven,
Might smile with scorn while raptured vision tells
Of the gay-colour'd radiance flushing bright
O'er all creation. From the wise be far
Such gross unhallow'd pride; nor needs my song
Descend so low; but rather now unfold,
If human thought could reach, or words unfold,
By what mysterious fabric of the mind,
The deep-felt joys and harmony of sound
Result from airy motion; and from shape
The lovely phantoms of sublime and fair.
By what fine ties hath God connected things
When present in the mind, which in themselves
Have no connexion? Sure the rising Sun
O'er the cerulean convex of the sea,
With equal brightness and with equal warmth
Might roll his fiery orb; nor yet the soul
Thus feel her frame expanded, and her powers
Exulting in the splendour she beholds;
Like a young conqueror moving through the pomp
Of some triumphal day. When join'd at eve,
Soft murmuring streams and gales of gentlest breath

Melodious Philomela's wakeful strain
Attemper, could not man's discerning ear
Through all its tones the sympathy pursue;
Nor yet this breath divine of nameless joy
Steal through his veins, and fan the awaken'd heart,
Mild as the breeze, yet rapturous as the song?

But were not Nature still endow'd at large
With all which life requires, though unadorn'd
With such enchantment: wherefore then her form
So exquisitely fair? her breath perfumed
With such ethereal sweetness? whence her voice
Inform'd at will to raise or to repress
The impassion'd soul? and whence the robes of light
Which thus invest her with more lovely pomp
Than fancy can describe? Whence but from thee,
O source divine of ever-flowing love,
And thy unmeasured goodness? Not content
With every food of life to nourish man,
By kind illusions of the wondering sense
Thou makest all nature beauty to his eye,
Or music to his ear: well-pleased he scans
The goodly prospect; and with inward smiles
Treads the gay verdure of the painted plain;
Beholds the azure canopy of Heaven,
And living lamps that over-arch his head
With more than regal splendour; bends his ears
To the full choir of water, air, and earth;
Nor heeds the pleasing error of his thought,

Nor doubts the painted green or azure arch,
Nor questions more the music's mingling sounds
Than space, or motion, or eternal time;
So sweet he feels their influence to attract
The fixed soul; to brighten the dull glooms
Of care, and make the destined road of life
Delightful to his feet. So fables tell,
The adventurous hero, bound on hard exploits,
Beholds with glad surprise, by secret spells
Of some kind sage, the patron of his toils,
A visionary paradise disclosed
Amid the dubious wild: with streams, and shades,
And airy songs, the enchanted landscape smiles,
Cheers his long labours, and renews his frame.

What then is taste, but these internal powers
Active, and strong, and feelingly alive
To each fine impulse? a discerning sense
Of decent and sublime, with quick disgust
From things deform'd, or disarranged, or gross
In species? This, nor gems, nor stores of gold,
Nor purple state, nor culture can bestow;
But God alone when first his active hand
Imprints the secret bias of the soul.
He, mighty parent! wise and just in all,
Free as the vital breeze or light of heaven,
Reveals the charms of Nature. Ask the swain
Who journeys homeward from a summer day's
Long labour, why, forgetful of his toils

And due repose, he loiters to behold
The sunshine gleaming as through amber clouds,
O'er all the western sky; full soon, I ween,
His rude expression and untutor'd airs,
Beyond the power of language, will unfold
The form of beauty smiling at his heart,
How lovely! how commanding! But though Heaven
In every breast hath sown these early seeds
Of love and admiration, yet in vain,
Without fair Culture's kind parental aid,
Without enlivening suns, and genial showers,
And shelter from the blast, in vain we hope
The tender plant should rear its blooming head,
Or yield the harvest promised in its spring.
Nor yet will every soil with equal stores
Repay the tiller's labour; or attend
His will, obsequious, whether to produce
The olive or the laurel. Different minds
Incline to different objects: one pursues
The vast alone, the wonderful, the wild;
Another sighs for harmony and grace,
And gentlest beauty. Hence when lightning fires
The arch of Heaven, and thunders rock the ground.
When furious whirlwinds rend the howling air.
And Ocean, groaning from his lowest bed,
Heaves his tempestuous billows to the sky;
Amid the mighty uproar, while below
The nations tremble, SHAKSPEARE looks abroad
From some high cliff, superior, and enjoys

The elemental war. But WALLER longs,
All on the margin of some flowery stream,
To spread his careless limbs amid the cool
Of plantain shades, and to the listening deer
The tale of slighted vows and love's disdain
Resound soft-warbling all the livelong day:
Consenting Zephyr sighs; the weeping rill
Joins in his plaint, melodious; mute the groves;
And hill and dale with all their echoes mourn.
Such and so various are the tastes of men.

Oh! blest of Heaven, whom not the languid songs
Of Luxury, the syren! not the bribes
Of sordid Wealth, nor all the gaudy spoils
Of pageant HOMER, can seduce to leave
Those ever-blooming sweets, which from the store
Of Nature fair Imagination culls
To charm the enliven'd soul! What though not all
Of mortal offspring can attain the heights
Of envied life; though only few possess
Patrician treasures or imperial state;
Yet Nature's care, to all her children just,
With richer treasures and an ampler state,
Endows at large whatever happy man
Will deign to use them. His the city's pomp,
The rural honours his. Whate'er adorns
The princely dome, the column and the arch,
The breathing marbles and the sculptured gold,
Beyond the proud possessor's narrow claim,

His tuneful breast enjoys. For him, the spring
Distils her dews, and from the silken gem
Its lucid leaves unfolds: for him, the hand
Of Autumn tinges every fertile branch
With blooming gold, and blushes like the morn.
Each passing hour sheds tribute from her wings,
And still new beauties meet his lonely walk,
And loves unfelt attract him. Not a breeze
Flies o'er the meadow, not a cloud imbibes
The setting Sun's effulgence, not a strain
From all the tenants of the warbling shade
Ascends, but whence his bosom can partake
Fresh pleasure, unreproved. Nor thence partakes
Presh pleasure only: for the attentive mind,
By this harmonious action on her powers,
Becomes herself harmonious: wont so oft
In outward things to meditate the charm
Of sacred order, soon she seeks at home
To find a kindred order, to exert
Within herself this elegance of love,
This fair inspired delight: her temper'd powers
Refine at length, and every passion wears
A chaster, milder, more attractive mien.
But if to ampler prospects, if to gaze
On Nature's form, where, negligent of all
These lesser graces, she assumes the port
Of that eternal majesty that weigh'd
The world's foundations, if to these the mind
Exalts her daring eye; then mightier far

Will be the change, and nobler. Would the forms
Of servile custom cramp her generous powers?
Would sordid policies, the barbarous growth
Of ignorance and rapine, bow her down
To tame pursuits, to indolence and fear?
Lo! she appeals to Nature, to the winds
And rolling waves, the Sun's unwearied course,
The elements and seasons: all declare
For what the eternal Maker has ordain'd
The powers of man: we feel within ourselves
His energy divine: he tells the heart,
He meant, he made us to behold and love
What he beholds and loves, the general orb
Of life and being; to be great like him,
Beneficent and active. Thus the men
Whom Nature's works can charm, with God himself
Hold converse; grow familiar, day by day
With his conceptions, act upon his plan;
And form to his, the relish of their souls.

THE END.

www.ingramcontent.com/pod-product-compliance
Lightning Source LLC
LaVergne TN
LVHW011223110826
845150LV00006B/1526

9781425516093